GETTING AND KEEPING NEW TEACHERS

Six Essential Steps from Recruitment to Retention

Janet D. Mulvey and Bruce S. Cooper

ROWMAN & LITTLEFIELD EDUCATION
A division of

ROWMAN & LITTLEFIELD PUBLISHERS, INC.
Lanham • New York • Toronto • Plymouth, UK

Published by Rowman & Littlefield Education
A division of Rowman & Littlefield Publishers, Inc.
A wholly owned subsidary of The Rowman & Littlefield Publishing Group, Inc.
4501 Forbes Boulevard, Suite 200, Lanham, Maryland 20706
http://www.rowmaneducation.com

Estover Road, Plymouth PL6 7PY, United Kingdom

British Library Cataloguing in Publication Information Available

Library of Congress Cataloging-in-Publication Data

Mulvey, Janet D.
  Getting and keeping new teachers : six essential steps from recruitment to retention /
Janet D. Mulvey and Bruce S. Cooper.
    p. cm.
  Includes bibliographical references and index.
  ISBN 978-1-60709-217-9 (cloth : alk. paper) — ISBN 978-1-60709-218-6 (pbk. : alk.
paper) — ISBN 978-1-60709-219-3 (electronic)
  1. Teachers—Selection and appointment—United States. 2. Teachers—Recruiting—
United States. 3. Teacher turnover—United States—Prevention. I. Cooper, Bruce S.
II. Title.
  LB2835.M85 2009
  371.1—dc22   2009022698

∞™ The paper used in this publication meets the minimum requirements of American
National Standard for Information Sciences—Permanence of Paper for Printed Library
Materials, ANSI/NISO Z39.48-1992. Printed in the United States of America

CONTENTS

PREFACE

Remember that wonderful nursery rhyme, "Finders, keepers. Losers, weepers"?

What's captured in these words can be applied to our schools. How can we find a great new generation of new teachers, help them adjust and grow, and keep them for years to come? They are our children's and nation's future.

It is the greatest challenge facing school leaders as they seek to recruit, support, reward, and ultimately retain new talent. Principals and other administrators must weep, quietly, when good new teachers leave, and those who struggled abandon education altogether.

Whether recently graduated or in a change of career, each teacher enters the field of education with an altruism and ideal for supporting and fostering our democratic way of life.

The stories and case studies in this book are authentic, taken directly from the experiences related to us by new teachers in the field. The names of persons and schools have been changed to ensure confidentiality of those involved and to protect from any personal reactions related to the studies.

The process of education is complex, involving factors of experience, socioeconomic circumstances, cultural diversity, resources, and the involvement of all stakeholders who benefit and contribute. We hope that the stories from some of those in the field will shed light on these complexities and help improve the education for all.

We wish to acknowledge and thank all the new teachers who enter our school systems dedicated to improving the lives of youth in this country.

①

INTRODUCTION: FROM TEACHER RECRUITING TO RETENTION—UNDERSTANDING NEW AND FAST-TRACK TEACHERS

> The fallacy of rationalism is the assumption that the social world can be altered by logical argument. The problem, as George Bernard Shaw observed, is that "reformers have the idea that change can be achieved by brute sanity." (Fullan, 1991, p. 96)

School leaders, teachers, and parents are all concerned about getting and keeping the best teachers for their schools. This book tells them how: what to do and what not to do. In particular, this book characterizes the qualities of schools in urban settings that either retain or discourage fast-track and new teachers from remaining in their school or the profession itself. The study looks at the qualities of these schools, including leadership, peer collegiality, student apathy, cultural understanding, classroom management, and resources for good teaching.

Evans (1996) relates a vignette of a principal at a conference on school reform: "Unable to contain himself, [he] burst out 'We've spent all morning discussing what changes are best. In my school, we have too many problems hurting too many kids. We need to change everything—now!'" (p. 3).

Many would agree, especially those who are working in high-needs schools in high-needs areas like inner cities, that they need extra help and support. Who is responsible for positive change? How is it accomplished and how can we stimulate growth in a system that examines and takes into account the many aspects of culture, community, socioeconomic strata, and experience in the educational arena?

This book is new and unique in that we make an ethnographic examination of key steps in teacher orientation in a real case study format from the field, in the words of teachers and leaders, as they attempt to build stable and effective schools. Each chapter outlines the characteristics and essentials of good schools and compares those characteristics to the actual environments in which new teachers work.

We take a long view, starting with the decision of many professionals to change careers and become teachers in high-needs districts. Through their own experiences and reflections, these teachers bring to life what it is like to work in climates that have qualities influencing them to remain in their schools or leave. Thus, this book is an essential resource for teachers, principals, community leaders, college preparation and new leadership classes, and anyone else interested in how schools work to build and retain a strong teaching staff. What we can learn from these detailed and real-life examples will help increase the stability of schools through better preparation and retention of teachers in real working and learning environments.

THE PROBLEM

Retaining new teachers has never been easy. And when the teachers are on the fast track for certification and placed in difficult schools, the problem of retention is even greater. Inner-city schools are desperate to find qualified teachers to fill classrooms, especially on the secondary level, and have initiated programs to answer the problem. While the number of recruits is initially encouraging, retention after the two-year commitment is discouraging. It is estimated that a mere 20 percent of those who enter the fast-track master's program remain in the inner-city schools.

Fast-track programs do recruit new education graduates, but the majority (67 percent) are change-of-career candidates and some older people reentering the workplace. Being accepted into the fast-track program is not easy; the qualifications for acceptance are rigorous. For example, in 2008 the NYC Teaching Fellows program had approximately 19,000 applicants and accepted approximately 2,500 (New York State Teacher Certification Examinations Web page, 2008).

Qualifications require an undergraduate grade point average of 3.0 and passing several standardized tests before being allowed to enter the classroom to teach. To help attract prospective students, the program offers scholarships for teacher training and college courses, a stipend for cost of living and a first-year teaching salary during the two-year stint in the program. So those who have chosen to enter and go through these rigorous requirements are dedicated people with the highest aspirations to teach and make a difference.

A typical program begins in the summer prior to the school year and immerses the candidates in courses and summer class work for six weeks. Following this intense orientation, the newly indoctrinated teachers are placed in full-time positions in schools. The experience they have and support they receive differ greatly from school to school and in most cases determine the success or failure of their effectiveness in the classroom, and their desire to remain in their current positions.

It is no secret that New York City schools, along with those in other inner cities, have been struggling with achievement gaps, low graduation rates, and higher than national dropout rates. The problems are well documented and reported in news articles, education magazines, and through other works of recognized authors. The schools most affected are those that reside in lower socioeconomic areas of the city. Poor physical facilities, lack of resources, and high turnover rates of both teachers and administrators add to the calamity of ineffective schools and unfortunately failing children. The new fast-track teachers are often placed in these ailing schools. Make no mistake about it, the fast-track teachers understand in advance that they will be placed in schools with high-needs students and will be working hard to help underserved populations receive a better education.

The failure of many schools to meet the demands of local, state, and national standards discourages many from entering the schools and committing to more than two years after starting in the fast-track certification process. In contrast, pockets of success are also occurring in areas with the same demographics in terms of culture and socioeconomic strata. Schools in these conditions have been more successful in retaining the novice teacher and improving the academic success for their students and are highlighted in this book.

The comparison of experience is so great that we highlighted the reasons for these differences that have not been studied and acted upon in all inner-city schools. Instead of the practice of closing failing schools only to reopen them under a different name and configuration, some inner-city schools and communities have come together to develop programs and environments where students are achieving success and teachers are fulfilling their professional desires to make a difference for their students and themselves. The reasons for the success, carefully documented through academic improvement and teacher retention, need to be examined and documented for discourse and change in all inner-city schools and beyond. The purpose of this study is to look at schools where fast-track teachers have been placed and to listen to their own words of frustration and elation, grasping and learning from varied experiences they have within similar demographic and ethnographic environments.

Fast-track teachers are enrolled in a course of study during their two years of commitment to the inner-city schools. They are obligated to remain in a placement (unless asked to leave by the building administration) if they wish to become certified with a master's degree. In at least two of their courses, they are asked to describe the demographic makeup of their school community. The information is designated for an analysis of how and why their schools perform well or poorly academically.

The community portraits give detailed information of the physical, academic, and leadership styles of the schools and describe the new teachers' experiences with staff, administration, and community. Some of the new teachers come from city environments themselves and have some knowledge of city life. In contrast, the majority of candidates (57 percent) come from suburban or more rural areas. Their induction into the city school environment is short and hardly representative before they enter the urban classroom.

The summer institutes, held for new teachers, prepare the novice teacher for the developmental stages of the students who they are going to encounter in the classroom and school and give them a quick overview of the subject areas they are interested in teaching. Methodology courses by professors in specific subject areas are reviewed for content and context. During the two weeks of course work in human development, they also are exposed to management courses from other fast-track teachers who have been in the field for one or two years. Their only classroom experience is the summer school environments that students elect to attend. In this short four-week period, they attempt to put into practice the information gained in their course work. The summer school classes are small and do not reflect the whole school experience.

Common to all case studies presented is the urban environment, demographic construct, and socioeconomic areas that the students come from. The population of students attending the schools is mostly black and Hispanic and qualify for free or reduced lunch programs. All are in the middle or high school years and the focus is on new fast-track teachers hired to teach math or Spanish. Some schools in the inner city reflect the neighborhood and draw students from that neighborhood while others are in neighborhoods that do not, in any way, reflect the area or residents.

ENVIRONMENTS AND RETENTION

The differences in the case studies are the environments in which the new fast-track teachers are immersed. The most notable differences encompass the leadership, peer collegiality, and support that exist within the walls of the schools. Physical conditions aside, the people who work within the academic community are the influences that help to determine whether a teacher will stay or go, remain enthused or be uninspired to teach.

Take, for example, East High School. In a description given by the East High School Official Review in 2006: "The school is housed in an old building and its facilities are cramped and dated and unable to cope with the demands of the modern curriculum and instructional delivery. The facilities need upgrading and are not conducive to support effective learning for teachers and students alike."

The school is situated in an area of housing projects and is almost entirely populated by black and Hispanic students living below the poverty line, who come from boroughs outside East Harlem. Robert, a fast-track teacher, describes the school as in desperate need of renovation. It has a computer lab that is not functional, an elevator that does not work, a library with no librarian, and windows that are fiberglass and nonfunctioning. The students in his class complain of the odor in the classroom and the crowded conditions.

Certainly, looking at the physical environment, one could hardly imagine a more depressing place to go to on a daily basis. In reality, the collegiality, leadership, and positive atmosphere generated by the staff within these dilapidated walls have moved the school from a failing grade of F to a B. Robert describes the traditions that are growing to show interest in the needs of the students outside the classroom that are positively affecting the overall academic improvement. Traditions include a Thanksgiving feast cooked by the staff for the students. Others include an annual ice skating trip to Central Park, an annual junior bowling trip, intramural basketball teams that compete against the staff, and finally a field day where all students can compete in various events.

The teachers are also involved in tutoring after school on a daily basis, resulting in improvement in Regents scores that helped raise the school to the B rating over a four-year period. The enthusiastic and can-do attitudes of this young staff have, according to Robert, "created classrooms that are misrepresented by the building. The classrooms are lively and energetic— fast paced and student achievement oriented." A regular needs assessment is the ongoing analysis that drives professional development for further improvement. The three assistant principals are supportive and involved in all activities of the school and have a goal of increasing their rating to an A.

Robert said, "I am proud to be an East High School Eagle, and I have fallen in love with the community around East, the faculty, and most importantly, the students. I could not imagine a better situation or a better environment for learning."

It is hoped that, with the new stimulus plan under the Obama administration, other high-needs schools can begin to mirror the experience of Robert, so that administrators, teachers, parents, students, and communities can respond to and benefit from a much-needed reform and renewal of the education system. Stephan Sawchuck (2009) writes that strategies in the new stimulus plan "can include induction programs to help hard to staff schools retain qualified teachers, improvement of working conditions in schools, and establishment of differentiated pay and other recruitment incentives" (n.p.).

The following chapters describe other schools with similar physical structures that have established environments that either support teachers in their quest to teach and learn or have fallen victim to the hopelessness that drives new teachers from particular schools or teaching in general.

The book examines the key qualities influencing those who stay in the inner-city environment and those who leave either the city or education altogether. Six environmental factors prove to be important to supporting and motivating fast-track teachers in their quest to become effective urban school teachers (see Lortie, 1975) and provide the structure and chapters of this book.

Effect of Leadership

The first factor is principal and assistant principal leadership in supporting new teachers in their classrooms and beyond. New teachers in general need direct help and support with the most difficult populations if they are to fulfill their duties and practice their craft. A vignette told by Angelo Patri (1997) about his first day as a teacher illustrates similar experiences by a number of fast-track teachers in the 21st century:

> Leading me to a classroom he opened the door and pushed me in, saying, "This is your class." Then he vanished. There were sixty-six children in that room. Their ages ran from eight to fifteen. They had been sitting there daily annoying the substitutes who were sent to the room, and driving them out of the school. The cordial reception I had been given by the principal held more of relief for him than of kindness for me. (p. 206)

Peer Support and Collegiality

New teachers also need role models and supporters, whether it is a teacher in the field or grade level, or another new teacher who is living through the same experiences and adjustment problems. Communication, sharing, and problem solving with colleagues, be they experienced or new, are crucial in reducing the frustration and feeling of isolation during those difficult first days.

Classroom Management

New teachers need to learn and perfect classroom management skills. From outside the classroom to the immediate environment inside the classroom walls, survival as a teacher often depends on establishing rapport with students, setting clear and acceptable expectations, and managing the day-to-day discipline in the classroom. Students need to know that teachers care about them but have high expectations for both behavior and academic effort.

Student Apathy

Student apathy is yet another area that needs to be assessed and ameliorated. Besides trying to manage students in the classroom, new teacher adjustment also involves overcoming the lack of student enthusiasm for learning, a personal effect of life in the classroom.

Cultural Differences

A crucial requirement for fast-track teachers is cultural adjustment, as apparently many of the fast-track teachers grew up and attended schools in rural or suburban areas of the country and only came to the cities to be trained and work in urban schools. This adjustment around lifestyle, class, race, and socioeconomic status may prove to be an important quality of teachers who "dig" the new environment, and those who find it off-putting.

Adequate Resources

Finally and important to curriculum delivery are adequate resources in the school and classroom. Most generally, new teachers commented on the importance of having what they need to teach well: computers, work tables, science equipment, textbooks, workbooks, and ample classroom furniture. How these teachers see themselves in a wasteland or an environment rich in resources has an effect on longevity and perspicacity.

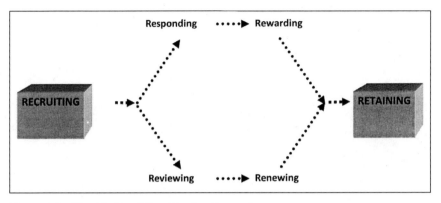

Figure I.I.   The Six Rs of New Teacher Retention

Together, and in different ways, these qualities are illustrated through case studies and personal ethnographic statements in the chapters to follow.

SUMMARY

Through the case studies and real experiences of new and fast-track teachers, around the previous factors, six essentials for retention are emphasized, as illustrated in figure 1.1.

The essentials of teacher retention not only take into account the initial motivation to pursue teaching as a career but also look at the whole environment, both the physical and the emotional, while reviewing and responding to the needs of new teachers, rewarding the efforts and successes, and renewing that initial motivation and altruism for life in the classroom.

2

WHO ARE THESE TEACHER RECRUITS?

The concept of teacher training in a set period of time—say, two, three, or four years—is misleading in its scope and meaning. Even teachers who have been in the classroom for many years will tell you that learning to teach is a career-long journey, constantly changing in complexity and meeting diverse students' needs. As Isenberg (1994) related in her chronicles of professional development after more than two decades, "Actually, the world of Smithfield High School only became comprehensible to me more than twenty-five years later, when I began to investigate the history of secondary English education in the United States" (p. 7). This insight only begins the journey and research of Isenberg and others into the complexity of teaching and learning in diverse cultural settings similar to the realities of life in city schools.

TRADITIONAL TEACHER PREPARATION

Most teachers come to their classrooms through traditional routes: that is, an undergraduate pathway that usually involves the study of liberal arts and sciences, and a master's degree with an emphasis in childhood, secondary, or special education. Trainees are given a half-year of classroom observation and then the experience of student or practice teaching. Mentoring and supervision are all supposedly part of the program with guided practice and direction before entering their own classroom domains. Even with this experience, and the ability to survive that first year teaching, a lifetime commitment to classroom teaching has declined over the past 10 years.

Due to prognostications concerning shortages of educators in the next 10 years, active recruitment has been ongoing to attract a growing number of change-of-career people into the field of education. Teachers now retiring after 25 years or more in the profession are leaving behind a world in education that will most likely retire with them. Several studies found that young aspiring teachers in the traditional programs, while enthusiastic to begin their careers in the classroom, do so with conditional attitudes toward remaining as classroom teachers for very long.

Haberman contended that teachers most likely to remain in the profession are those who are older and more experienced in life (Quirk, 2008). Through his research and experience, Haberman suggests that the younger, newer graduates entering the classroom have little life experience that can relate to the issues and complexities of today's students, especially those who live in poverty.

These newcomers are open to the possibility that they may want to change their original intent to stay in the classroom or change direction altogether. Shannon, a college student who had a successful high school career in a suburban setting on Long Island and is currently finishing her fifth year in a teaching college in Connecticut, has already changed her mind about different positions in the education field.

She is enthusiastic about the possibility of having her own classroom and an opportunity to make a difference in the lives of young children. At the same time, she is pragmatic and states forthrightly, "I am not married to the profession. If I don't like it, I will do something else." Thus, whether she will remain in the field as a lifetime commitment is very much up in the air. The job stability of educational professionals, in particular the classroom teacher, is a cause for concern in the nation's education system and alternatives are being tried to fill these crucial positions in a range of fast-track, accessible new ways.

Teachers who come to the profession through a less direct route, such as making a change of career, often have worked in another field but have only experienced the classroom in their own primary, secondary, and tertiary education paths. Haberman supported this trend and wrote, "For children in poverty, success in school is a matter of life and death and they need mature people who have a great deal of knowledge about their subject matter but who can also relate to them" (cited in Quirk, 2008, n.p.).

For these new but more mature prospective teachers, the much-needed direction, mentoring, and primary support that are part of the traditional preparation program are often absent from their training. So where do these prospective teachers come from and what do they need?

Dan Lortie (1975), a sociologist who has studied the work of teachers, coined the term "apprenticeship of observation" to describe the knowledge we obtain about teaching during the years we watch our own teachers from kindergarten to high school graduation. He believed that in many ways those school years are like "serving an apprenticeship in teaching" (p. 61). But unlike a traditional apprenticeship, which usually pairs one novice with one master craftsman, learning about teaching from the 12 years you spent in classrooms as a student is unscientific and biased by personal experience.

HISTORICAL BACKGROUND

History can be greatly enlightening when studying the pathways of new teacher selection and training. The national perspective and belief in the educational system for democratic growth have developed over time. Education and public schooling began in the 1630s when the only criterion to teach was the ability to read and write. Formal training for teachers did not emerge until the 1800s and was dominated by males since females were given little opportunity for higher education and instead attended two-year normal schools before entering primary school teaching. Interestingly, many males used the profession as a stepping-stone and moved on to other areas for better pay and opportunity.

Females who were allowed to teach were poorly trained and often began in their teens. Once the prospect of marriage emerged, they were required to leave the profession. It was only in the 1840s, after Horace Mann became the first secretary to the Massachusetts Board of Education, that teacher preparation was focused upon as an essential reform for quality in the classroom. Mann also became a supporter and activist for women's rights of access to higher education and entrance into the classroom. It was through his efforts that the first normal schools were created to train teachers for their jobs in the classroom. Tozer, Violas, and Senese wrote, "Mann correctly understood that fundamental to the problems that he and others observed with common (public)-school teachers was the inadequate preparation most teachers had received" (2002, p. 59).

The normal school was the first institution designed specifically to train teachers. "Rather than encouraging the incorporation of teacher education into existing institutions, Mann opted for new institutions that would be different . . . one developed where the pedagogical methods were not only included in the curriculum but dominated by it" (Tozer et al., 2002, p. 66). With support from educational reform advocates such as Henry Bernard and Horace Mann, the number of normal schools increased rapidly during the latter half of the 19th century.

At the time, Mann was not concerned that teaching be recognized as a profession. Rather, he was concerned that an adequate number of practitioners, with necessary skills, be trained to provide a high-quality education to the growing number of students entering the common schools. It was mainly a matter of supply and demand.

It is important to note, however, that the normal schools focused on elementary education with emphasis on the psychology of child development. "Preparation for secondary-school teaching, which demanded a larger academic component, was left to liberal arts colleges. Training for secondary-school teachers remained primarily a function of liberal arts colleges until after World War II" (Columbia Encyclopedia, 2007, p. 46785).

At the dawn of the 20th century, John Goodlad noted that "teaching still fell short of professional status . . . that two year normal-school curriculum provided poor professional preparation . . . and, that knowledge it presented was ill-defined, unscholarly and submissive" (1984, p. 287). And as Sayas (1996) remarked, "Such characteristics do not fit well with the preparation of a professional capable of autonomous practice based on specialized expertise" (p. 8).

The normal schools expanded into four-year teachers' colleges and were, at the time, training a substantial number of the nation's public school teachers. The requirements needed to enter one of these institutions were modest at best. During this early, 19th-century time of recruitment, it was only necessary to convince a local school board of exemplary character and moral standing before a new teacher was hired. Some states did require a candidate to pass a test for admittance, but it was generally one of cursory knowledge.

By 1867, according to Ravitch (2003), "most states required teachers to pass a locally administered test to get a state certificate, which included not only the basic skills, but also U.S. history, geography, spelling, and grammar" (n.p.). The 19th century brought nonstandard approaches to teacher certification, including subsidized academies that prepared teachers for schools. The normal schools begun in Massachusetts for the elementary years later incorporated longer periods of time for preparation; and teacher training organizations delivered by hiring teacher trainers experienced in the field of teaching. Although efforts were being made to train teachers for the common school, no single standard existed and teaching was not recognized as a profession as such.

The 20th century was, perhaps, the beginning of recognition for more intense and standardized teacher preparation. "A development that came about was the attachment of teacher preparation programs to four year baccalaureate degrees, such as law and medicine had at the time" (Ravitch, 2000, pp. 287–288). The new four-year programs became a combination of theoretically based understanding, pedagogical methodologies, and curriculum knowledge. The demise of the two-year normal school occurred, as teacher education programs were located in teachers' colleges and universities around the nation.

What remains the same as in Horace Mann's time is the need to recruit and retain highly qualified teachers in our schools. The attraction to teaching has long been an issue, as teaching is reputed to have a lower incentive for intellectuals or those interested in a highly professional career. The media focus on the poor education of our youth and the comparison and ranking among countries around the world do little to inspire prospective candidates to enter the field of teaching. Tozer et al. (2002) remarked:

> In the spate of educational reform reports, discussion of the professionalism of teaching always begins with concern for the quality of schooling. Once it is established that education in schools is deficient, it is a logical step to hold teachers responsible for it. If there are problems in schooling, it is asserted, they are due in part to inadequacies among the teachers. (p. 290)

This type of reporting does not invite qualified people to enter a field where blame is placed on schools and teachers without examining all the other factors that affect outcomes and learning as a nation. As Goodlad (1976) wrote of the critical subject:

> Education is a never-ending process of developing characteristic ways of thinking and behaving on the part of individual, nations and mankind. Each generation has access to a long heritage from which to derive its perspective. Its thinking is shaped by current books, magazines, and newspapers: by movies and television; and by a kaleidoscopic array of events and stimuli which are part of everyday life. Schooling—elementary, secondary and higher— constitutes the most planned and ordered but not necessarily the most influential part of the process. (p. 6)

Perhaps the most damning criticism about schooling in America was the Holmes and Carnegie reports in 1986 that focused not only on the ills and lack of competitiveness in the nation's schools but also recommended some key ideas for improving teacher preparation for future classrooms (Tozer et al., 2002). Among the recommendations were five criteria to address the quality and licensing of teachers:

1. To make the education of teachers intellectually more solid.
2. To recognize differences in teachers' knowledge, skills, and commitment in their education certification and work.
3. To create standards of entry to the profession—examinations and educational requirements—that are professionally relevant and intellectually defensible.
4. To connect our institutions to schools (for teacher preparation and development).
5. To make our schools better places for teachers to work and to learn.

The political and economic response to the report was mixed, embraced by critics concerned about the state of education and deplored by those in the field as well as in many colleges and universities. What the report accomplished was a new examination of teacher recruitment and preparation and the debate of how to attract and keep the best teacher talent for our schools.

The debate rages on and is summarized by Ravitch (2003) as follows:

> Our nation faces a daunting challenge in making sure that we have a sufficient supply of well-educated, well-prepared teachers for our children. There is surely widespread agreement that good teachers are vital to our future. However, there is not widespread agreement how we accomplish this goal. (n.p.)

BACKGROUND TO INCENTIVE

It is now an opportune time to recruit and train new types of candidates to be the nation's teachers. The current downward trends in business and industry and the outsourcing of skills to other nations have made teaching look more attractive. Salaries and benefits in public education appear stable and job security more promising than current trends in other private-sector markets. The attraction to teaching can carry many marketing incentives that were absent 20 or 30 years ago. The basic principle of supply and demand shortages has opened alternative pathways to certification and has made those pathways more attractive.

An introduction to career ladders in teaching has become more viable and attainable. Teachers who have the incentive to continue in education can become staff developers, building administrators, chairpersons in their subject areas, and leaders in higher education. The possibility of district-wide appointments that influence school reform locally, statewide, and nationally can be pursued through easily accessible higher learning institutes.

Paid tuition for certification, stipends for cost of living, and a short commitment to the district or areas assigned, while the certification process is pending, attract those who are in between jobs or are searching for new careers. The past dedication to a single chosen career has diminished and people find themselves open to new career opportunities. This mobility has put a strain on the education system, as even those with a traditional pathway often do not remain in teaching for a lifetime, but it has also opened the door for many other candidates who did not initially chose education as their career.

The change-of-career candidates who enter the field are considered more mature and settled in their ideals and expectations. After all, they have managed a career, thus understanding the complexities of social structure and experiencing the highs and lows of the workplace. Some have stayed at home to raise a family and now are free to pursue a career outside the home. These new teachers provide the needed resources to cover classrooms and to fill the future vacancies in America's schools. It is also hoped that these candidates who have already experienced other routes and have satisfied some of their wanderlust will find that education is indeed their calling.

In her report at the White House Conference on teacher preparation, Ravitch (2003) suggests that some barriers to potential excellence in the classroom be removed. She complains that the current standards may be hurdles that do not truly assess the quality of teacher potential. Specifically, she questions "whether we are talking about the kind of standards that will produce more effective teachers or about the barriers that are simply hoops and hurdles intended to screen people out of the profession who have not taken courses or degrees that have no relationship to being a good teacher" (n.p.).

CASE STUDIES

Many change-of-career teachers come to the field from various backgrounds with the idea of giving something back, making a difference in kids' lives, and helping change the societal structure for struggling urban schools. Eric, a teaching fellow in his second year in the program, has found a niche that at this time is most fulfilling and exciting. A doctorate holder and a former college adjunct professor, Eric is teaching in an urban school with a large immigrant population. The low socioeconomic status of the student body is evidenced by 100 percent of the students receiving free or reduced-price lunch. His enthusiasm for the school and the students is seen every week as he completes his alternative certification.

Susan entered the program after several years of child rearing with the expectation of giving advantages to inner-city students that her child has had in his school. Her teaching experience in her school has proven to produce a mix of both positive and negative feelings toward the school in general and the program instituted for the students. Susan has the maturity to look at the situation in a more pragmatic way and to compare the influence of politics and administrative efficiency with the results of the program. She remains dedicated to her role as a teacher and plans to continue but not necessarily in her current placement.

John, a digital graphic designer, came to teaching after deciding that his work in the periodical newspaper industry was unfulfilling, and he wanted to explore other options. His pursuit of certification and the opportunity to teach is a stopgap while he examines other possibilities for a lifetime career. His experience in school placement has been less than positive, driving him even faster from the field to seek other avenues. Unfortunately for both education and John is the fact that he began with a positive attitude and would be giving more time if the climate were supportive and encouraging.

Brendan, a quiet older individual, comes to teaching from the business sector and is dedicated to his new career. His deep reflection on the needs of inner-city students and the belief that he can make a difference will sustain him in persevering to find the correct placement within the system. In midterm his assignment was changed and he was placed in a classroom outside his areas of expertise or knowledge. His failure to adapt quickly enough to a special needs assignment forced him to resign to avoid being let go by the principal of the school.

Without training or supervision, he was unable to meet the program criteria for special needs youngsters. He said, "I was sorry to have been put in a position where it was necessary for me to resign from working at this school. A little more support by one administrator somewhere, a guiding hand, or an extra week to get up to speed is all I would have needed to stay and become part of this wondrous worthy enterprise."

Bruce is using his time as an alternative certification teacher to learn a new skill while saving to pursue his career in physics. With a business background, teaching is his second venture on his road to a third master's degree. Bruce was highly critical of his placement in an inner-city school, but with his own initiative and an influx of new teachers in this expanding school, he has found his place and support. Bruce is highly inquisitive and interested in the students' well-being. He feels that his second year has been much more fruitful and successful than his first. He has been given a little more leeway in developing his program while adhering to the necessary standards. He feels more successful and, although he still plans to pursue physics, he may remain a little longer in the city public school system as a teacher.

NEW RECRUIT EXPERIENCE

In the haste and need to fill the many vacancies that exist, especially in high-needs schools, the new recruits, not so wet behind the ears, need as much if not more of the six essentials for retention to maintain their sense of worth and efficiency as those who have had the experience of mentoring and student teaching.

In a report by the National Commission for Teaching and America's Future (1996), a new focus emerged that looked not only at the professionalization of the teaching profession itself but combined the efficiency and skill of teaching with student performance. The commission, while comprehensive in its findings, began with three premises:

1. What teachers know and can do is the most important influence on what students learn.
2. Recruiting, preparing, and retaining good teachers is the central strategy for improving our schools.
3. School reform cannot succeed unless it focuses on creating the conditions in which teachers can teach, and teach well.

If we are to retain new teachers, regardless of their avenues to the classroom, we must begin to make sure that they are valued, if they are to be valuable, supported, encouraged, and guided with new ideas so that perhaps they will give as much time as possible to the classroom and students.

SUMMARY

New teachers are needed now and more new recruits will be required in the near future. Sustaining a viable education system is in the national interest if we are to keep pace with the rest of the world. Teachers are the essential force that makes this possible and if we are to retain them, we must examine our current practices of recruiting and retaining.

The traditional preparation program for teachers from undergraduate to master of science in teaching has not changed that much over the last 20 years. While programs have advanced and adjusted to satisfy the existing curriculum, the process itself remains pretty much the same. The amount of time spent in teacher training and experience pales in comparison to the apprenticeship in other professional fields. Doctors and lawyers, for example, spend up to two years under mentorship and guidance before actually practicing their craft. Teachers, even in the traditional educational pathway, get as little as six months in the classroom before becoming responsible for educating our youth. The alternative pathway to teaching gives prospective teachers as little as six weeks. This lack of classroom experience and mentoring places all new teachers in situations that can be overwhelming. One year of stress and uncertainty can be a catalyst that results in a quick exit from the classroom. Munby, Martin, Russell, and Martin (2001) observed:

> That it is probably not as easy as it seems: As many have noted, intending teachers' prior experience of teaching is severely restricted. Although they have observed thousands of hours of teaching behavior, they have not been privy to the profound and extensive knowledge and thinking that underlies this behavior. As with any good performance, good teaching looks easy. When we witness a near-perfect performance in, say, the long program of a figure skating competition, we recognize the many hours of intensive work that lie behind the apparent ease of execution under demanding circumstances. But we typically do not do this of teaching. (p. 895)

Alternative programs have been put in place to ensure that our schools have the teachers they need to run their programs and educate the youth of tomorrow. The alternative pathway has recruited some very talented change-of-career personnel and attracted a number of those who are exploring their options for future employment. The alternative program does not have the same support and experience foundations that the traditional pathway supplies but can provide support and guidance to ensure success for the recruit and the students. Haberman insisted, "It is necessary to recognize that most of what effective teachers learn they learn on the job from mentors, colleagues, and self-reflection" (cited in Quirk, 2008, n.p.).

The retention of alternatively certified teachers has not been promising. But even those who have completed the more traditional program and experience are leaving more rapidly than ever in our history.

If history is the greatest teacher, we will examine the research on the educational process for both teacher and student. We must gather evidence that supports practices on solid and valid research. Universities and colleges must come out of their isolated towers, become involved in school classrooms, and develop their own knowledge on teacher and student learning. As Goodlad states about one of his major goals for American schools, "an individual's satisfaction in life will be significantly related to satisfaction with her or his job. Intelligent career decisions will require knowledge of personal aptitudes and interests in relation to career possibilities" (1984, p. 56).

It is incumbent upon all who work in the public school systems to develop a support system within the school environment to mentor and partner with dedicated individuals who have talent and desire to teach. This book tells how, using real-life situations as data and new frameworks to use these cases effectively.

❸

PRINCIPALS' ADMINISTRATIVE LEADERSHIP: SUPPORTING NEW TEACHERS IN THE FIELD

Educational leadership can be madness or it can make a contribution to improve our schools. It can be a frantic effort to fix everything or it can be concentration on a few important items. It can be a futile exercise of power or it can empower individuals to help themselves. In the face of dramatic social change, conflicts over governance, and excessive demands made on schools, it can be said that one who aspires to school leadership must either be mad or a supreme egotist.

WHY SCHOOLS LOSE FAST-TRACK TEACHERS: SAD TALES

This chapter follows the path of fast-track teachers and their experiences in schools that have similarities in their physical environments, serve students who live near or below the poverty line, and serve communities that are not necessarily connected to or supportive of the school. The effects of poor leadership on the school, peer collegiality and support, interest in student achievement beyond the dreaded assessments, resources, and student attitudes, reflect an atmosphere that has lost the intention of teaching and learning. Johnson (2007) supported the concept of disillusionment of teachers who are attracted to the field of teaching for "the love of learning or the delight of working with children" due to responsibilities that lack the educational flavor and due to lack of support from competent school leaders (p. 33).

NEW TEACHERS' NEEDS

What new teachers need is sustained, school-based professional development, guided by expert colleagues. Principals and teacher leaders have the largest roles to play in fostering such experiences (Johnson & Kardos, 2002). Problems in schools and in education in general can be persistent, but are especially well documented in high-poverty areas exacerbated by poor early preparation and failure to meet the bureaucratic standards set by government policies. Failing schools are basically located in high-needs areas where poverty is rampant and the communities are unresponsive to educational issues.

The type of leadership needed to promote change is discussed in many research articles. But it is the teachers who see and feel the consequences of poor leadership and can articulate direct experiences of that lack of leadership, which, in too many cases, determine whether or not they remain in the school or education in general.

It is no secret that good leadership usually results in successful schooling. Understanding and responding to the culture of a school is imperative if the school is going to motivate its teachers and students. Affecting the teachers' lives means giving support, mentoring, and power to effect the changes needed for success.

Educational leadership, unlike leadership in business and industry, is subject to complexities that involve success of human beings, not products or goods and services. The success of humans includes the students, teachers, parents, staff, community, and society. There are no simple formulas for leaders to follow, no blueprints. School leadership requires the mantra of personal unselfishness, of dedication to the individual, the group, and the social community.

Theories of leadership cover many areas and complexities. The following are but a few examples of the most prominent theories for social evolution and the inclusion of the human element in schools:

- The formation of ideas
- The articulation of ideas
- The building of ideas

Included in these ideas of building a community, transformational leadership, according to Conger (1996), incorporates several stages and is a process that involves and includes the recognition of the human side of the school environment:

1. Being sensitive to constituents' needs, seeing current problems as opportunities, and building a vision that addresses them.
2. Articulating this vision in a way that simultaneously makes the status quo unacceptable and the new vision appealing.
3. Establishing trust among followers through proof of sincere commitment to the vision.
4. Showing the means to fulfill the vision, including the setting of their own personal example, the empowering of others, and the use of unorthodox methods (p. 169).

Authentic and transformational leaders establish trust among their constituents and are visible, while visionary, and supportive in the changes that take place in the school and the classroom. The leader's behavior exemplifies the commitment that is expected from the staff and students in the school. Evans (1996) explained, "The importance of setting the example, of leaders modeling what they value, is one of the most frequently repeated themes in leadership writing. Authentic leaders translate their beliefs and values into concrete actions at the fundamental level" (p. 189).

CHANGING PERSONAL PRACTICES

Historically, teachers with experience and seniority often request and are given classes with the fewest problems, with the most accomplished students, in the most interesting courses to teach. For example, in many high schools advanced placement courses are instructed by senior teachers, while newcomers are left with the more challenging, most poorly behaved, and difficult students at basic levels. Thus, the problems of new teachers are compounded by their regular assignments. As one former high school department chair reported, "I gave difficult classes to the most experienced teachers in the school, and assigned some new teachers to advanced placement courses. It worked!"

The following cases demonstrate the qualities of leadership that determine whether new teachers remain or leave the school or the teaching profession. The influence of leadership on new and seasoned teachers can be the major reason for success or failure of the teacher, the student, and the school.

CASE STUDY I: B. L. HIGH SCHOOL

The B. L. High School is located in a more affluent New York City neighborhood, bordering 84th Street between Columbus and Amsterdam. The
student population attending the school belies the wealthy look of the area.
The demographic of the school is noted as 63 percent Hispanic/Latino and
34 percent African American. The culture of the school is undisciplined,
evidenced by the fact that according to John, a first-year fast-track teacher,
there are 10 arrests weekly.

A 2002 report by the *New York Times* revealed that during that same year
the New York City dropout rate averaged 20.4 percent, a slight increase
from the year before. B. L.'s average for the same year was 36 percent.
Reasons given by Chancellor Levy were the fear of failing the Regents in
mathematics and English. In 2007 the graduation rate hovered at about
38 percent while daily attendance was approximately 65 percent. In an
annual accounting of high school noncompleters nationwide (American
Youth Policy Forum, 2002–2003), 20 percent of students from low-income
families dropped out of school, sadly compared to an even higher number
at B. L. These statistics represent the challenges that fast-track teachers
are confronted with as they enter the doors to their schools and their new
chosen career.

Leadership and Its Importance

John is a change-of-career candidate who worked in the computer digital
world for several years. He is math oriented and entered the fast-track program to gain a master's in secondary education with a focus in mathematics.
He has completed his first year in the fast-track program with excellent
grades academically but with disheartening experiences in his school placement. College classes deal with theory and methodology, history and prag-
matics; but experiences in the school and classroom are the most powerful
teacher of all. Principals in schools have the power to make or break the
sustained motivation and desire to teach, regardless of the socioeconomic
status of the school and students.

Statistically, principals and administrative leaders have the capacity to
improve student learning. Although the gains are relatively small, according
to a published report by AERA, Leithwood, and Riehl (2003), "Leadership
explains about three to five percent of the variation in student learning. . . .
This effect is actually nearly one-quarter of the total effect of all school factors." Poor leadership can, then, reduce the capacity for student learning

and achievement. The inability to galvanize a staff or encourage positive qualities through modeling and demonstration has a deleterious effect on the climate of a school or department within the school. Invisible administrators who closet themselves in the principal's office can have little positive effect on the teaching team.

Fast-track teachers are in need of ongoing supervision, encouragement, and feedback if they are to succeed in the first two to three years in the classroom. Principals and assistant principals need to be in evidence in hallways, cafeterias, classrooms, and recreation areas throughout the day. Good leadership is crucial for success and a sense of adequacy for all teachers in the school environment, but it is fundamentally vital for the first-year fast-track and new teacher. Six weeks in a summer program with (promised) monthly mentoring from an outside supervisor is a calamity waiting to happen without almost constant attention from an experienced and dedicated administrator in the school.

John's Story

John accepted the position at B. L. High School based upon the encouragement of his fellow advisor and because the Department of Education had rated the school as satisfactory. From his observation, however, the rating is "nothing more than a slip of paper." The constant fights and lack of achievement among most of the students are deleterious in the environment that permeates the school. (The litter accumulated during the day is evidence of the lack of respect for the school environment.) The presence of rats and roaches creates a working and learning environment both unappealing and unworthy for students and staff alike.

School leadership and principal strength are essential in building a community that is safe and that focuses on the students' needs for achievement. A study done and reported by Marzano and McNulty (2003) outlined the effect of leadership on the school and student achievement. Principals in school set the tenor and direction in building learning communities by connecting the physical plant with the needs of all constituents in that plant. Efficiency, dedication, academic rigor, and student demeanor can be predicted as soon as one enters a school building.

Let us experience the daily life of a new fast-track teacher whose enthusiasm to teach is confronted with the daily realities of life in a high school that has high turnover in teachers and poor leadership to innovate and inspire change. The outside façade of B. L. High School is attractive and seemingly well kept. Inside, the picture is more dismal and threatening—including metal detectors and security personnel to prohibit weapons from being carried into the building. Hallways are washed daily of the graffiti that is imposed on them, but graffiti remains prevalent and ignored in the bathrooms, away from public view.

The students wear "do-rags" and other gang-related headgear and clothing. The occasional rat and roach are visible mainly on the fourth floor of the building, and air conditioning is operational on two floors and nonexistent on the other two. Classrooms are windowless and cramped, housing 35 students each, an illegal count for the size of the rooms. B. L. High School, created from a former IBM manufacturing facility, has the infrastructure to support excellent computer services and climate control, but is in disrepair due to lack of updating and focus from the school administration.

The large facility has all the space necessary to engage students in extracurricular activities: gymnasiums, a music room, counseling offices, vocational shop area, art rooms, science labs, and even a garden room. Physical possibilities abound for engaging and motivating student interests and achievement; yet the statistics reveal a school failing not only in engagement of students but in academic accomplishment and new teacher retention.

According to John, the staff consists mainly of new and fast-track teachers along with some hard-core staff who have remained due to their inability to procure other placements. The lack of personal attention from the principal is documented by the amount of unsatisfactory evaluations given by the administration. John reports that he met with the principal once on October 30, 2007, and finally gave up trying to meet with her again, after daily requests for such a meeting failed for several weeks. His survival at B. L. depended on the psychologist in the building, who listened and supported him, allowing him to vent his frustrations and doubts about his ability to teach in the environment.

The fear, according to John, that is instilled by the principal has affected all personnel in the building. The principal dominates meetings with descriptions of all the positive things that are happening in the school. Issues and concerns are not allowed to be mentioned or addressed. This constant state of discomfort, lack of communication, and the plethora of poor evaluations by the principal resulted in a planned protest among the staff. Out of 90 teachers, only 6 attended these meetings. An inquiry as to why meetings did not receive more support revealed that most teachers are untenured and those who attain seniority leave the school.

John's personal experience of receiving an unsatisfactory evaluation is as follows. A math teacher, he was switched from regular to special education due to staffing needs. Lacking any training in special education and with no support from the administration, John admits to his difficulty in adjusting to the needs of the students. He assessed their needs through his own design, developing a program based on the levels determined through the assessment. Following a one-time observation, he received an unsatisfactory evaluation from his principal. Unable to arrange an appointment to discuss the evaluation, John met with his union representative, who advised him not to pursue his dissatisfaction, as it most likely would result in dismissal.

The result of one year at B. L. High School brings into question whether John will become one more statistic in the loss of teaching talent in the inner-city schools.

CASE STUDY 2: BEDFORDS HIGH SCHOOL

Margaret, who works at Bedfords High School, observes similar structural deficiencies but dissimilar commitment to the students on the part of teachers. She describes the oppressed feeling that her students have in a white affluent neighborhood. Lack of assimilation might factor into the poor attendance (70 percent) and the resulting continued plummeting of state Regents test scores.

The inability of the administration to understand the culture of the student body has also resulted in programming that does not engage the students or create effective strategies that help them assimilate into the culture of academics. Margaret expresses complete frustration at the fragmentation of programs, isolating subjects as entities instead of integrating them. Margaret describes the administration, principal, and assistant principals as noncommunicative with one another or with the teachers in the school. Scheduled meetings are rarely held and those that do take place are poorly organized and planned and in general ineffective and uninformative. "To be frank," Margaret says, "there is no purpose to education at Bedfords High School, besides memorizing material that does not relate to my students' lives."

Margaret's evaluation of the teaching staff is not complimentary. She describes her colleagues as persons who are more interested in appeasing the administration than in helping their students. Their classrooms are bright and cheery with pictures and bulletin boards that please the administration but are empty of content and context. Many of the teachers are described as devoid of motivation to understand an interdisciplinary curriculum and seemingly depressed under the circumstances of their lives at school.

The administration—unable to understand the concept of teamwork, shared goals, and visions—has exacerbated a difficult situation. Most teachers who remain are those who cannot find placement anywhere else or are comfortable with an environment with little or no supervision. As for Margaret, she loves her students but feels she would be more effective in a living, learning organization.

CASE STUDY 3: MANHATTAN HIGH

Manhattan High School is located in midtown in Hell's Kitchen. Eric, finishing his first year in the environment, is excited about the outcome of this year and is looking forward to the commencement of year two.

The physical structure and its shortcomings are similar to many conditions in the inner-city environment. The building, erected in 1972, consists of cement blocks lined with lockers and, according to Eric, "has a utilitarian feel with no ambiance or message about learning." A large structure, it has been divided to accommodate five schools, with no access to a library, physical education facilities, or spaces for art and music.

The student population is almost exclusively Latino, recent immigrants with no connection to the area of the school's location. As a result, the school staff and administration make every effort to create an atmosphere of community within the walls of the building. A report of students' economic status in 2005–2006 showed that 81–90 percent of families received public assistance.

Response by the students to the community endeavor is both positive and rewarding. They are proud of their school, as shown by the lack of graffiti anywhere in the building and the attendance at Saturday sessions that offer tutoring in English and key academic subjects. The creative elements integrated into the program help to ameliorate the lack of library or physical education facilities. Enthusiasm is evident among the whole learning community, thanks to a principal who has had experience in building teams of teachers and learners. Eric describes his principal as "masterful at creating nonintrusive partnerships."

She plans her budget carefully and encourages field trips that add to the cultural experiences of these newcomers in our society. The social justice and caring at the school are also evidenced by setting high standards with the objectives of sending as many students as possible to higher education institutions. The principal of Manhattan High School is planning, according to Eric, to find the funds necessary to give students help in their first years at college.

Leaders in public education do not inflict standards and prescribed programs on their staff but work cooperatively with their faculty in creating shared visions, goals, and outcomes that are student centered. This principal has established an environment that has energized the staff to give extra time and effort to build a high school that meets the needs of all students. Of the 11 new teachers, out of a total of 27, all have expressed their desire to remain for the coming year.

CASE STUDY 4: KAPLAN INTERNATIONAL

Kaplan International is one of six schools that are housed in R. S. High School in the Bronx. The original school was closed in 1996 due to failing test scores, violent activity, and a general malaise as an education facility. The restructuring that occurs when a school is shut down is not a new concept but often a flawed one. Schools that have not made adequate yearly progress for two consecutive years can be shut down and then reopened under a different name with a new principal but without the structural changes often necessary for success. Fortunately, that is not the case with Kaplan. One of the six smaller schools opened in the past year in the old R. S. High School, Kaplan is housed in one corner of the building and is being led by an experienced principal who is creating an environment that is organized for learning.

Ravitch and Viteretti (2000) asserted that teachers in all schools, especially those who work in city schools, must know that they will receive recognition and support in their initial assignments. Professional development should address the specific needs of the school and the environment and not be subject to the marketing of prescribed programs that are not applicable to the situation.

Kaplan International has been created with such a mind-set and is slowly developing an environment that is supportive, congenial, and respectful to all who work and study there. The physical environment exhibits portraits and work of the students. Uniforms and high expectations for behavior and academic effort have helped set the tone. Mozart's music is the signal to change classes and continues during passing time in hallways. Aulecia, a new teacher in the school, contends that the other five schools, once critical of these initiatives, have now begun to adapt their own programs in a similar manner.

The principal holds morning meetings every day to welcome the students and announce the day's news and events, establishing a sense of community for staff and students alike. She instituted an earlier start to the school day so that students who travel from Harlem and Washington Heights, a 30-minute train ride, can avoid the crush and rush of the morning commute. There to meet them as they enter the building are the staff and the administration, demonstrating the care and concern displayed in their mission statement.

Aulecia states that most of the teachers in this small startup school are new first- and second-year novices, hungry for the experience and motivated by the charge. In a personal interview with her principal, the following mantra was expressed: that teachers are in the business of cultivating global citizens. She asserts that most children want to learn and it is up to the teacher to use materials that are respectful and rigorous in instruction and provide the best we can give.

SUMMARY

As Kouzes and Posner (1987) asserted, "The true force that attracts others is the force of the heart" (p. 125). Thus, real leadership in a school requires a relationship with staff based on honest engagement, fair and unbiased evaluation, and common pursuit of organizational and academic goals. The examples of hubris in the first two case studies invite failure in engagement of staff and the likelihood that those who began with the best intentions to initiate change in inner-city schools will be lost to that school or to a career in education altogether. For principals who are leaders in name only, the possibility of creating or instilling valued relationships among staff and developing sound academic programs for students is dubious at best.

Fast-track and new teachers begin their experiences with a minimum of course work and classroom training. They expect and should receive support from colleagues, administrators, and other experienced staff. Being thrown into an environment that is more foreign than familiar without support is tantamount to throwing a nonswimmer into 10 feet of water without a life jacket. School leaders who simply impose goals and use punitive measures when those goals are not met are incompetent in establishing a working, learning organization that benefits all within the community and can cause failure among many new fast-track teachers. It is the ultimate responsibility of leaders in a school to know their staff, support and encourage their strengths, and assist them in the learning process. Only with visionary and supportive administrative leadership will inner-city schools close the revolving door and retain their teachers.

Good leaders—those with vision and the skills to motivate, support, and create learning environments—have the propensity to develop followers and collaborators in even the most difficult schools. It is within their power to help fast-track teachers become effective in a relatively short amount of time. Good leaders understand the environment, have empathy for new inexperienced teachers, and believe that together, administration and faculty can team to help students learn. School leaders create conditions that allow their staff to succeed. They are data driven for efficacy in curriculum and environmentalists in providing the climate needed to exercise the academic necessities and beyond. Atkinson (2007) remarked, "We have to listen to the voices of teachers when they talk about working conditions and need for mentor support. We must, through a systems approach, help them to change instruction to prepare students for worlds we cannot imagine" (n.p.).

4

PEERS WHO CARE: COLLEGIALITY, TEAMWORK, AND BEYOND

Teaching is often a lonely activity, where teachers work behind closed doors, and rarely visit each other or share materials during the school day. For experienced, effective teachers, this isolation may be fine, although even these professionals might enjoy interacting with peers as they teach— although team teaching has peaked and disappeared in most schools, because everything was results oriented and teachers had little time to consult with each other. Also, some districts found team teaching expensive, since teams of teachers had to relate their respective subjects to sets of core objectives, and some teachers found that frustrating and difficult. It was hard, sometimes, to make math and English integrated or connected, so each teacher retreated to his or her room and got on with the business at hand.

Teachers, like their students, have different professional needs and learning styles, and school leaders, to help them survive, need to tailor the orientation of new teachers to particular conditions and learning styles. As Guskey (2000) explained, "Because participants often have different learning styles or preferred learning modalities" (p. 33), they require different approaches to help them grow and survive as new teachers. Kennedy (1998) "found that the greatest effects were obtained when teachers were engaged with knowledge directly relevant to what students are learning" (p. 125).

Goals for new teachers fall into three areas: cognitive goals, psychomotor goals, and affective goals (see Shulman, 1986). New teachers need to understand these categories and set their cognitive goals, which relate to "understanding of the content they teach" (Guskey, 2000, p. 124). They should learn certain psychomotor skills (actions) such as setting up the school classroom and materials, and then mastering the ability to engage students in discussion and cover the curriculum. Guskey wrote, "Psycho-motor goals typically involve participants' ability to use the content in new and different contexts, make application when necessary, and determine the effectiveness of implementation efforts" (p. 125).

Finally, affective goals "are the attitudes, beliefs, or dispositions that participants are to develop as result of a professional development experience" (p. 125). New teachers thus need to develop their cognitive behaviors, those that teach students and build cognition, along with how to work the classroom (the psychomotor goals) and the right feelings and beliefs to make their job work, and to help them survive as new professionals.

Thus, for experienced, more knowledgeable teachers, peer support is helpful but not essential. But for new teachers, peer interaction may allow them to learn their craft and be interested in remaining as teachers in their schools. This chapter—on the themes of finding and retaining new teachers—explores the role of peers that can help particularly in the retention of new staff. Few teachers know how best to teach before they start. Thus, they learn on the job by doing—and need help in adjusting and prospering in the classroom. Thus, peer support, it turns out, is critical to helping neophytes to learn the craft and art of teaching.

This chapter explores the role of peers in support of new teachers, how they help mentor newcomers or remain isolated in their classroom and provide little or no support to those entering the profession. Often the survival of the new teacher depends on the support that can come fork peers and leaders within the school environment..

POSITIVE CASE: BUILDING A COMMUNITY

Kaplan International School, located in the Bronx, is small and unique, a place where teachers are called professors and students are called scholars; the school is brand new and enjoys a high attendance rate of around 90 percent. Thus, all the teachers are in a sense new and have built peer relationships that support the newer teacher as well. The school's goal with a diverse student population is to prepare students for the high school New York State Regents exams by bringing them to grade-level performance. The vision at Kaplan is preparation for the world, in a global sense of where students are now living and will be living in the future.

Implicit in Kaplan's goal is the desire to see students succeed beyond high school, in a world larger than the Bronx. Students take a rigorous set of courses, including the usual math and English, science, social studies, and music—plus Chinese and the theory of knowledge. This language and philosophy was designed to give students a global view of their education and their future.

The facilities are poor, including a shoddy setting and unusable rooms even though the school was built to accommodate a large population. In fact, Kaplan is one of six individual small high schools located on the same premises as a large high school that accommodated over 5,000 students before its closing in 1996. Of the six small schools, Kaplan is the most recent, with 300 students.

However, the sad environment may actually be a stimulant for the staff of this small school to pull together and support each other. Within the last two years, Kaplan took its small portion of the building and immediately began to create a bright and welcoming environment mainly by painting the walls and rearranging the furniture. Student portraits, green plants, and other decorations cost little, but made the place a happier school.

Starting the Year Together

To establish the desired learning community at Kaplan, teachers and staff worked hard at the beginning of the year to welcome all students and to set high work standards for themselves and the students. Students are required to attend school in a uniform and make a true commitment to Kaplan, because with a 7:30 a.m. starting time and long commutes from all over the city, students must rise early and leave home by around 6:30 a.m.

Since school starts early in the day and the commitment is high, Kaplan has been able to waive the demeaning security search and the use of metal detectors—again demonstrating to new teachers that the school trusts and respects the kids, and the kids feel the same about each other and the staff.

Beginning the Day Together

Every morning, the school holds a town hall meeting for everyone, starting at 7:30 a.m., to make the day's announcements, recite the Pledge of Allegiance and the Kaplan pledge and mission statement, and allow time for students or teachers to share concerns and discuss issues of interest. This open forum is a way of building team spirit and handling problems before they become too difficult.

One example is the need to make last-minute changes in locations and schedules because of the overcrowded conditions and the requirement to share facilities with the five other schools in the building. The challenges are daunting. But instead of giving up, staff and students have risen to the occasion. It is not uncommon to find a Chinese language class being conducted in the hallway because of a conflict in the use of rooms and the unavailability of the library and conference room.

The issues and concerns on the agenda in the morning often lead to a general discussion among both new and experienced staff, giving the newcomers a chance to hear what the senior professors advise, and thus building a collegial environment. For example, when a science teacher quit before the school year began, the problem was discussed among the whole faculty, and two of the professors agreed to take turns giving lectures until the new teacher arrived—thus students did not fall behind in the curriculum.

Thus, the newer teachers witnessed the dedication of the staff and realized that education has its emergencies, and that everyone can rise to the occasion. This spirit of togetherness permeated the school and helped build relationships among professors.

Ending the Day Together

The staff of mostly first-year teachers often stayed until 6:00 p.m. and met together collaboratively or tutored their students after school. This can-do attitude and full-day commitment from 7:30 a.m. to 6:00 p.m. were both signals to the new teachers that everyone was there together, and the days were long enough to meet, chat, and handle problems and improve the curriculum. This longer day is in stark contrast to the more typical time frame in which teachers are required by union contract to work a five-period day, of no more than about four and a half hours, since each teaching period is by contract only forty-five minutes.

In all, then, first-year teachers found Kaplan to be a stimulating, forceful environment where everyone pulled together, met early and late, and committed themselves to teach each other and to be problem solvers together. Everyone from teachers (professors) to administrators and staff involved in making key decisions have helped the new teachers to feel part of the community and to understand the complexities of running a learning environment. Teachers hire teachers, watch each other teach, and ask questions of new candidates.

Thus, Kaplan seems to enjoy continuity, and teachers (even new ones) want to remain there to help build the community of the school. For as the school year drew to a close in 2008, the teachers shared their reflections on what went well, how things might be made better, and what the new year might hold. As one new professor explained, "I already know that I'm going to have my first project planned out much more thoroughly, rubric and all, for next year. I realize what I must do better and differently next year." This planning indicates a willingness to stay and grow, and not run and hide.

Another new teacher lamented about his lack of organization skills. He explained, "Even though I'm not well organized, I did okay this year; but I could have managed my curriculum with focus and clarity." This admission of weakness and desire for future growth shows a self-confidence and a belief that colleagues will help and not condemn a new teacher.

NEGATIVE CASE STUDY: SOUTHSIDE VOCATIONAL SCHOOL

This case involves an older, more well-established vocational school that has witnessed high teacher turnover. Southside Vocational School is located in an area of the city that is generally considered nice, with fancy stores and good restaurants. Those who inhabit the neighborhood often make six-figure salaries and live in apartments above the trendy shops. However, one area of this neighborhood is mostly forgotten and houses Southside, home to 975 high school students.

It is clear to the passerby that this high school is an unwanted site, a weak part of the community, and a low-class presence in the neighborhood. Students who attend the school do not blend in with the shoppers, tourists, and residents, but hang out in the public park across the street from Southside, smoking, lingering, cursing, and occasionally fighting with each other. The nearby delicatessen has banned all the students from their premises, and people walking by tend to stare at pregnant teenage students and the teenage boys who wear their pants halfway down their buttocks.

Unfortunately, the community outside the school does not understand the teenagers who attend Southside Vocational. Not only do the students come from different racial and class backgrounds, they often speak little or no English, which is the main language of this affluent neighborhood. A local newspaper, the *New York Sun*, stated, "it is not often that a pack of violent teenagers looking to pilfer candy and chips from stores overruns the streets of a well-heeled neighborhood." Further, the story explains that these teenagers once caused a near-riot—with one member of the community saying, "There was a huge pool of people; it was so frightening" (Satow, 2005).

Thus, the environment around Southside is not supportive, and conditions within the school itself are not much better. Disorganized leadership, poor communications, and confusing organization structure, three of the problems at Southside, combine to make the school a formidable place for new teachers, and one that sees high teacher turnover.

Disorganized Leadership

First, Southside Vocational School suffers from confusing and weak leadership, creating a poor environment for new teachers to receive help and guidance. The school is divided into three separate learning communities, each with its own leader. These divisions are based on vocational areas, such as art, business, and technology. An assistant principal, working under a principal, heads each community. The problem, it seems, is that the three assistants cannot communicate with one another—nor do they answer to the principal.

The meetings of the whole school are poorly organized and uninformative. Because "the three academies divide teachers up into small 'learning communities,' vertical alignment within academic subjects is nearly impossible" (as reported by a Southside teacher). Thus, not only do the administrators disagree and fight, but also the subject area staff are not working together to align the curriculum and ensure that students are learning in an orderly way.

Subject area meetings, for example, are scheduled once every few weeks, but are often canceled or never happen. As one new teacher explained, "My colleagues are entirely preoccupied with appeasing their superiors, rather than engaging students in learning and helping each other." Administrators at Southside Vocational do not usually understand how to make the program more engaging and fail to grasp the complexities and interdisciplinary nature of collaborative education. For this reason, many teachers are unfocused, isolated, and fragmented in their teaching.

Confusing Communications

Southside Vocational also suffers from weak to nonexistent communication and collaboration among teachers. One teacher said, "I am constantly frustrated by seeing my students go through their day thinking that English is completely separate from global history and earth science. . . . Most teachers in my school stray from what I believe is a most vital part of teaching high school: constructing a continuity of interdisciplinary subjects. From what I have seen, most other teachers break up content with projects, book work, presentations, and collaborative learning—which is not part of our environment."

For these reasons, students are not able to grasp the material, nor can they really comprehend the continuity, the major themes, and their education as a whole. One teacher states, "Education consisting of memorization for the purposes of test taking has no interest or application to my students' lives and results in little motivation to learn."

Another teacher, sadly, said, "Because my school does not have teachers that work together to build a community of education continuity, we cannot adequately help students achieve the American dream."

Teachers themselves seem depressed with their lives, according to one observer. Either they used to be good teachers but are now burned out, or they were never very good but were rather lazy and knew that they could get by with poor teaching at this school. Thus, new teachers have no role models, or even have negative ones. Observers report that teachers do not care much about student achievement or understanding, but rather only care about their own student pass rates of standardized tests.

Roundly stated, "teachers do not promote social justice because they do not care what is right for the student; they care more about how their classroom looks from the outside."

These qualities together explain why new teachers leave, and old teachers hide in the classrooms.

SUMMARY AND THE FUTURE

As this chapter shows, peer involvement and support can make or break a school, and explains in large part why new teachers either stay and thrive, as in the case of Kaplan, or run and hide, and leave as soon as possible, as in Southside Vocational School. Peers matter. They set the tone and environment in schools and play a large role in building or destroying the process of recruiting, training, and retaining new teachers in American education.

Locating and sustaining quality teachers, as this book shows, involves six steps, which we call the six Rs of teacher retention: (1) recruiting quality new teachers; (2) responding to their needs; (3) reviews that are helpful; (4) rewarding and recognizing teachers who have grown in their work; (5) renewing their spirit and skills to build stronger teacher confidence and understanding; and (6) retaining quality teachers in schools.

Six Rs of New Teacher Retention

1. Recruiting	→	2. Responding
3. Reviewing/Understanding	→	4. Rewarding/Recognition
5. Renewing	→	6.Retention

Guskey (2000) has found that professional development activities are critical to school improvement and teacher adjustment and longevity. He wrote, "The kind of organization support needed for a workshop or seminar, for example, may be quite different from what is essential for study groups or *peer coaching*. That is why discussions of organization support and change are so vital in the earliest stages of any professional development endeavor" (p. 152). So, the process of keeping new teachers follows the six steps.

Step 1, recruiting good teachers: With shortages in some districts, school districts need to pay attention to finding quality teachers, in sufficient numbers and support them throughout their initiation into the school/learning process. The four intervening steps are important, in order to retain teacher and to create a stable environment within our schools. Research shows that "teacher quality—as measured by test scores and the proportion of teachers with masters' degrees—and class size appear to affect learning" (p. 280). But these assume that teachers are adjusting to their work and will remain as teachers in the future.

Step 2, responding: This chapter shows the importance of the school and its leadership being focused and responsive to the needs of new teachers, starting even before the school year begins (Glassman & Glassman, 2007).

Step 3, reviewing and understanding: Regularly reviewing and understanding the new teachers' needs and growth are regarded as critical to new school improvement. Feedback is the key: not critical or threatening, but showing understanding and being helpful.

Step 4, recognizing and rewarding: These have been shown to be important for new teachers. Complimenting them on their work, giving them much-needed recognition for the their accomplishments, and helping them to communicate what they are doing to other new teachers, and more seasoned ones too, are key steps in sustaining and retaining them.

Step 5, renewing: To ensure that new teachers won't quit or give up, leaders need to renew their teachers' spirits, knowledge and growth—giving feedback and more time for reflection.

Step 6, retaining these teachers: We need to track the careers of teachers, to follow their preparation, for as Hoy and Hoy (2006) wrote, "Increasingly the research suggests that the key to improving student learning rests with what happens in the classroom: the teacher is critical. Instructional leadership calls for the principal to work with education teacher colleagues in the improvement of instruction by providing a school culture and climate where change is linked to the best knowledge about *student learning*" (p. 3).

In sum, keeping new teachers remains a fundamental problem in the United States. While the current economic recession may mean that teachers need jobs and are less likely to leave, the data over the last 30 years are rather disturbing, as so many teachers leave the profession. As Glickman, Gordon, and Ross-Gordon (2007) found, "Novice teachers tend to have more negative attitudes about themselves, their teaching, their profession, and students at the end than at the beginning of their first year of teaching. Between one-third and one-half of teachers drop out of their profession within their first seven years of teaching (Metropolitan Life, 1985) with up to 15 percent leaving each of the first two years" (p. 26).

It is hoped that building a peer-oriented, supportive teaching community will sustain teachers, provide them the support and skills, and cut the dropout rate of these new teachers. We need to communicate what we are doing to new teachers and help them talk to each other. Glickman et al. (2007) explain, "Generally, people in schools do not talk about their work—*teaching*—with each other. . . . Talk is generated through faculty and committee meetings, in-service workshops, observations and conferences, faculty lounge contacts, and other informal occasions" (p. 28).

As reported by Sam Dillon in the *New York Times*, many of the nation's new teachers are quitting because of poor pay and bad working conditions; meanwhile, Dillon found that the other end of the career path, the highly experienced, are also leaving the profession because of enticement from the New York State retirement system—leaving in their mid-fifties. Thus, the newcomers are not being helped by the veterans, and the old timers are not finding a new role for themselves as mentors and models for these recruits. As Dillon (2009) explains:

> To ease the exodus, policy makers should restructure schools and modify state retirement policy so that thousands of the best veteran teachers can stay on in the classroom to mentor inexperienced teachers. Reorganizing schools around learning teams, a model already in place, in some schools, could ease the strain on pension systems, raise student achievement, and help young teachers survive their first, often traumatic years in the classroom. (p. 54)

This chapter shows that talk needs to be more deliberate, concentrated, and useful to new teachers, as they come to work and learn in a school community. The leader's job is to nurture that community and help the new teachers to thrive (Goodlad, 1984) among their peers. The legacy of the one-room schoolhouse is gone, and a new "professional community model" is required, where dialogue is ongoing within a "shared professional culture" (Glickman et al., 2007, p. 28).

5

UNDERSTANDING STUDENT CULTURE: CAN ANYONE TEACH THESE KIDS?

Back in 1932, George Counts wrote in his classic study, *Dare the Schools Build a New Social Order*:

> Like all simple and unsophisticated people, we Americans have a sublime faith in education. Faced with any difficult problem of life we set our minds at rest sooner or later by appeal to the school. We are convinced that education is the one unfailing remedy for every ill to which man is subject, whether it is vice, crime, war, poverty, riches, injustice, racketeering, political corruption, race hatred, class conflict, or just plain original sin. We even speak glibly and often about the general reconstruction of society through the school. We cling to this faith in spite of the fact that the very period in which our troubles have multiplied so rapidly has witnessed an unprecedented expansion of organized education. This would seem to suggest that our schools, instead of directing the course of change, are themselves driven by the very forces that are transforming the social order. (1995/1932, p. 278)

"I try, honestly, I do. I try to get my students to work in groups, to use problem-solving skills when working out a problem. I have even demonstrated multiple ways to get to the same answer. Graphic organizers, vocabulary drills, journals are all the tools necessary for students to become independent learners but have failed in my classroom. My modeling is met with groans and my insistence that they use strategies to find alternative methods for solutions is met with resistance. 'Why can't we just do math?' is the chorus of my students."

This is a typical response of new teachers when confronted with constructivist models in a master's education class. Patrick Finn's (1999) *Literacy with an Attitude* describes the type of teaching delivered in schools of the low, middle, and affluent socioeconomic strata in our society. While Finn places blame on the system, stating that expectations for poor and minority populations are lower and without challenge, perhaps we need to look at what precedes these expectations and how we might prepare for different outcomes. Is there a reason for delivering different types of teaching to different strata in the economic spheres? Our new teachers propose that it is the cultural expectations in their classroom that demand direct, teacher-centered learning for students who reside in culturally influenced areas.

Finn, Freire (1970), and Dewey have each described the "banking system" of teaching. Teachers instruct, and students listen and regurgitate the facts and statements delivered in the classroom. This system of teaching and learning has long been criticized for its bias as an instructional model. Books, articles, and journals have long criticized the lack of higher standards and better thinking models for those who reside in the lower socioeconomic strata of society. Blame has been cast on teachers and schools for delivery of the traditional mode of instruction. But is it a disservice to students to deliver modes of instruction that are foreign to their cultural background? How does cultural influence determine how we might approach curricula that have been systemized and made uniform for all students?

Why do new and many seasoned teachers who work in the diverse cultures of our system cite the failure of the professional development programs that promote the constructivist approach to learning for their students? What are the reasons why students fail to respond to the attempted approaches that should motivate and engage learners in their own learning? Can it be that the majority of teachers in our inner-city schools are white and have no real knowledge of what makes up the cultures in which they work?

Public schools in the inner cities and increasingly in many of our suburbs are, in fact, experiencing an influx of black (African American, Caribbean, etc.), Latino, Hispanic, and Asian students. As our schools become more culturally diverse, our teachers in general are having some difficulty connecting with the students and providing adequate instruction. Ford and Whiting (2008) commented:

> despite the changing demographics that make our public schools more culturally and linguistically diverse and the growing body of knowledge on issues of diversity and difference, multicultural teacher education continues to suffer from a thin, poorly developed, fragmented literature that provides an inaccu-

rate picture of the kind of preparation teachers receive to teach in culturally diverse classrooms. (p. 52)

Classrooms in our colleges and universities continue to teach methodology courses with practices that mirror researched models of collaboration and constructivism. No one would deny that these methods can be effective with large numbers of students who are culturally accustomed to the constructivist model. But many students who are recent immigrants or are culturally disposed to the authority of the teacher have difficulty adopting this methodology. As R. K. Vogel (1998) pointed out, "Students of diverse backgrounds and social conditions, language and dialects now populate our schools, a situation that we would have thought unusual a decade ago. Demographics tell us that most of these children are culturally and linguistically unlike the majority of teacher candidates, teachers, and administrators" (p. 18).

Inner-city schools have seen children from all over the world enter their classrooms with different languages and very different experiences in schooling, from formal and stable instruction to sporadic and sometimes no experience with schools of any kind. According to the Department of Education, the graduation rate among these new immigrants was just 29 percent in 2007. While cities and communities struggle to absorb these students, programs to help them in classrooms have yet to be developed.

We need to understand the frustrations that these student encounter that cause stress for the teachers who meet them in school and for the students who have little guidance in negotiating the system. John, a second-year teacher, complains, "These students don't even try." Educated in a wealthy suburb outside of the city, John is having his first real encounter with people very unlike himself. He tries to compare their lack of assimilation with the large wave of immigrants from the early 1900s. He strongly supports the current educational standards and the mandated assessments. His lack of training and support in dealing with immigrant issues are expressed as blame on others. John will not remain in the city but has said he will try to find a position elsewhere.

CASE STUDY: BRUCE

Bruce works in a school that houses 100 percent black, African American, and Latino students. His proficiency and love of math are clearly expressed in his collaborative planning, learned in graduate-level courses. He is innovative, knowledgeable, and motivated in attempting to engage his students in the learning process. Bruce states, "My students are more focused, and engaged, with prescribed textbook type lessons, that are traditional and limited, rather than in discovery and explorative activities." The students seem more content, less stressed, and better behaved when working with concrete algorithms, in contrast to problem-solving strategies.

Bruce has taken staff development and university classes that promote a constructivist model of engagement, exploration, discovery, and collaborative effort to solve math problems. He has taken these to heart as the way that he was taught in his middle-class suburban schools. His students rebel against the format and respond with, "Mister, this isn't math, this is reading." When Bruce explains that they need to know how to do both to pass the state Regents test, he is met with a lack of interest. His attempt to vary lessons with a combination of concrete and abstract principles has, in his opinion, failed in his classroom. Bruce, in his second year, has reflected on reasons why his delivery is not successful. His assessment of the students' attitude and proficiency has resulted in a two-pronged evaluation, first that his students are unprepared in the basics of numeration, and second that they have deficiencies in reading and comprehension skills. The combination of the two results in a failure to communicate the level of proficiency necessary for success.

Bruce also teaches a health class, where students are given the opportunity to relate to current health issues, where interest should be more personally relevant and subject to discussion. But, in fact, they would rather have work sheets with prespecified questions and answers. The frustration of attempting engagement with innovative plans and creative thinking, only to be dissuaded by lack of student response, is discouraging to teachers who have learned in a different way and have been conditioned to teach in a manner familiar to their learning and teaching style.

Another of Bruce's frustrations is a lack of understanding of why his students do not seem to want to learn. An enthusiastic student himself, Bruce cannot conceive why interest is lacking and apathy is apparent. He states that his students are "stupid," not in terms of intelligence but in their general indifference to the aim and promise of an education. Bruce's attitude toward his students has become increasingly negative, and although he continues to seek the door that will open their minds, he feels that he himself is inadequate to teach.

Bruce has indicated that he will finish this school year, but plans to leave the school and the profession to pursue a career in physics—another good teacher lost.

Learning and understanding cultural differences in behaviors and expectations are crucial if teachers are going to be successful in classrooms where their own paradigms of teaching and learning are in direct conflict with those of their students. Many of the new immigrant families—or those who have been isolated in their communities—have expectations that schools are the institutions that are responsible for training their children to be ready for the future. Others blame the families and schools for not doing their jobs and allowing students to fail and drop out.

Du Bois (2006) has referred to racial subordination as a major reason that minority students perform poorly in schools. In the early 1960s, cultural deficit theory studies "blamed the child's social, cultural or economic environment as being 'depraved and deprived' of the elements necessary to 'achieve the behavior rules (role requirements)' needed to academically succeed" (Hess & Shipman, 1965, n.p.). The stigmas placed on students who are newly immigrated or from impoverished circumstances define them as unmotivated learners or unintelligent. What teachers identify as lack of interest and/or apathy is defined within their own biases and lack of understanding of the needs and wants of those different from themselves.

CASE STUDY: SUSAN

Susan works in a school where all of the students come from communities outside of the school's neighborhood. The conflict between the population of students and the community is so strained that shops and retail establishments have banned the students from the premises. Students have been prohibited from the local delicatessens and food markets at lunchtime due to "fear of vandalism and stealing." The sharp contrast of the demographic makeup in and outside the school can be compared to the difference between "black and white, affluent and poor."

In conversations with several parents who have students attending Balfour High School, Susan reported that they did not seem to mind that the school is dilapidated and in great need of fundamental conditions for health and safety. Perhaps, she reports, they are accustomed to these conditions and see no contrast.

The way that students view themselves is a direct response to the way they have been designated by those in power (socioeconomic). Erikson, a cultural sociologist, pointed out inadvertent misunderstandings among the cultures and said that "teachers and students play into each other's cultural blind spots." And it is a fact that an individual's family, cultural background, and neighborhood influences have an effect on students' learning. Feelings of esteem, self-worth, and potential are a direct result of status in the family and success in school. When schools present curricula in a uniform way without recognition of an individual's beliefs and basic principles, they reduce the possibilities of success. Guild (1994) asserts:

> Schools are heavily biased toward uniformity over diversity. An appropriate balance must be determined thoughtfully with attention to beliefs, theories, and research rather than efficiency. We need to decide intentionally what should be uniform for all students and what should be diverse. And strive toward putting into practice what we should believe. (p. 16)

CASE STUDY: JEROME

Jerome, a bright and dedicated teacher, works in the Bronx in a newly formed school that is intended to attract committed and quality students from across the Bronx. The school has the hope of establishing a reputation that will attract students of all cultures, but, to this point, the school is still segregated with few white students. Located in the Bronx among some of the most crime-riddled projects, according to Jerome, it fits Jonathan Kozol's (2005) paradigm of a completely segregated school with few of the resources needed to succeed.

In a school focused on math and science, Jerome has been responsible for creating an information technology service at the school. In an effort to determine Internet access, Jerome did a survey to learn about the availability of service. The community, which includes many housing projects in a low socioeconomic area, has no Internet access and, with a median individual income of $12,932 and a family income of $32,172, many students do not own a computer. The more salient features of the demographics and location offer more evidence of cultural deprivation and blindness to the needs of the population.

The significant crime rate in the projects spills over into the school community. Jerome complains that while most of the students come from the same neighborhood, many of them reside in the same buildings and have strong connections to their block. When a rift occurs between the school and an individual student, that student usually falls back on his or her connection to the neighborhood.

Jerome reports that while the demographic of the student body reflects the neighborhood in which the school is located, the staff all reside outside of that neighborhood. As a matter of fact, most of the teachers and administrators live outside the borough, creating a divide and lack of understanding of the daily influences of the students' community. The racial difference is also worth mentioning, with the students being mostly black and Hispanic and the teachers white.

The following incident recounted by Jerome is just one example of how cultural differences affect students' ability to relate and to learn. The principal of the school observed a student throwing a book at another student in the hallway. The thrower was brought to Jerome for discipline. Jerome spoke to the young man, who first denied, then admitted and apologized for the incident. Jerome asked the student to apologize to the principal. "John agreed and dragged his feet back to Mr. C. where he muttered an 'I'm sorry.'" Mr. C., according to Jerome, is a towering black man who dresses impeccably and is somewhat intimidating to the students. Jerome expected that he would accept the apology and return to work. Jerome was surprised and impressed at the reaction of this black man to his black student: "Sorry? Sorry doesn't cut it. Did you know that for many years people said, 'If you want to hide something from a black man, put it in a book'? Look at yourself! What are you doing now?"

Jerome was enlightened and embarrassed that he thought a simple apology would suffice. He realized two very important things: one, that Mr. C. was able to access the commonalities of race as a motivator for proper behavior, and two, that the essence of the crime was not the throwing itself, but what was thrown. Jerome witnessed a commonality that was able to cut to the heart of an issue with a young black male at the school.

Another incident reported by Jerome gives us a view of poor minority students' possible perceptions of the "white man." Jerome was accompanying his class back from a field trip when one of his more assertive students began doing an impersonation. While waving a piece of paper, the student changed his walk to become more stilted and proper. "Look at me—I am walking like a white person! I just got my paycheck," he shouted. Another student in the group began to copy him and others joined in. "Wait a minute," one of the students shouted. "We don't have to copy him. We have a real white dude, right here. Mr. Jerome."

As they joked and laughed, the students continued to "walk like a white man" for most of the trip home. Jerome was amused and troubled at the same time. What were their impressions of the white man? Did they center on success and financial security? Where are the successful minorities in

their neighborhood to imitate and look up to? When education levels reflect similar trends to the socioeconomic status of the neighborhood, with
less than 66 percent graduating from high school, how do we teach them
the value of education?

CULTURE AWARENESS

One of the most important factors in teaching students of all cultures is to
instill in them a positive image of themselves within their own cultures and
neighborhoods. Only after that can we expect them to develop the integra-
tive quality that participates and contributes to society at large. Ladson-
Billings (2001) asserts:

> The average white teacher has no idea what it feels like to be a numerical or
> political minority in the classroom. The persuasiveness of whiteness makes
> the experience of most teachers the accepted norm. White teachers don't un-
> derstand what it is to "be ashy" or be willing to fail a physical education class
> because of what swimming will do to your hair and although African American
> youth culture has become increasingly popular, and everyone can be heard
> saying, "you go girl" . . . the amount of genuine contact these teachers have
> with African Americans and their culture is limited. (p. 81)

Have teachers who work in areas that are culturally different from their
own blamed deficiencies in learning on the specific culture? Can it be that
without indoctrination into the beliefs and traditions of those cultures that
we mistake differences in learning styles for deficiencies? Samuel Brown,
director of the Youth Foundation in Harlem, strongly advocates that teachers who work in a community get to know their community intimately. His
workshops include educators who live and work in Harlem and who em-
phasize that success for teacher and student means familiarity with family
life, beliefs, traditions, and expectations. The ability to form relationships
with students and families beyond the classroom makes the connections
essential for learning and understanding.

It is rare that the majority of white teachers have a well-versed understanding of other cultures. They have been raised and educated in segregated communities and for many, the only exposure to other cultures has
been through the media or excursions into cities that exemplify diversity.
Their views of diverse students are limited and their motivation to help
"these poor underprivileged children" is beset with misconceptions. Teachers who are truly knowledgeable about their own uniqueness as individuals

within their cultures are better prepared to help their diverse students become knowledgeable about their own cultures and proud of their uniqueness. They do not ignore or attempt to change the traditions, beliefs, and
customs of the population they are working with, but know how to honor
those customs and communicate with their students. Students who are re-
spected for their connections to the community and their cultures are more
likely to feel good about who they are, where they are, and how successful
they can become within and outside of their own environs.

CASE STUDY: KATIE

Katie works in a high school in East New York, Brooklyn. The demographic
of the community is composed overwhelmingly of blacks, West Indians, and
Latinos. The median income level for the immediate area that supports the
high school is $25,597, according to the census in 2004. The area, once a
high-crime, crack-infested neighborhood, is left with rundown living quar-
ters, few retail establishments, and few amenities for the population.

According to Katie, the school, built in 1923, is in a state of extreme
disrepair. Scaffolding has been placed around the school for renovation,
but nothing has been done since the scaffolding was erected. The school is
infested with rodents and has remnants of bullet holes left over from the
violent period. The school is not handicapped accessible and does not meet
requirements for physically challenged students. The environment of the
school reflects the condition of the neighborhood, and the students' attendance and proficiency match both.

The school motto, "No excuses accepted," attempts to set the tone and
expectation for the student body. The students themselves make excuses in
all areas of the academic program: lack of homework completion, disrup-
tion in classes, and refusal to take the mandated tests ordered by the state.
Only a few students excel, and the Principal's Wall of Excellence boasts only
a handful.

The school has 21 full-time teachers, ages ranging from 22 to 32, many
of whom work outside their areas of certification. Although the teachers are
dedicated and motivated to promote social justice and academic proficiency,
the needs of the school, community, and the students are overwhelming.
Teachers at the school believe that students in the community "can move
on to better things" and encourage them to seek options outside of their
neighborhood. Many of these students, according to Katie, never venture
outside their Brooklyn neighborhoods and are not experiencing anything

beyond their own front door. They encourage students to take advanced placement and summer classes but to little avail.

Creating caring classrooms at the school has proven to be most difficult. Most offenses other than fighting have no consequences, establishing an atmosphere of fear, frustration and chaos within the school community. Students have united against the establishment, are combative with their teachers, and are constantly wary of anything presented by the establishment. They refuse to take tests, truly engage in the academic program, or collaborate in the learning process. Their attitudes reflect past failure, and their defenses guard them from being labeled as dumb or stupid.

Katie reports the school has done little to reach out to the community, offering no fund-raising activities, holding no programs to advance communication between home and school, and only reporting negative behavior on the part of students.

How can teachers believe in the intellectual capacity of students when they are beset with problems that need the whole village to pursue and deal with? How do colleges and educators encourage teachers to become culturally competent? What lessons can be learned from the cultural divide of the white teacher in the minority school?

Educators know that students learn in different ways. They have been acquainted with programs and workshops on learning styles, differentiated learning, cognitive styles, and inclusive classrooms. In all cases, regardless of cultural propensities, a uniform agenda of curriculum has over taken our society: a one-size-fits-all routine.

In *Marching to Different Drummers* (1998), Pat Burke Guild and Stephen Garger quote Nathaniel Cantor's book: "The public elementary and high schools, and colleges, generally project what they consider to be the proper way of learning which is uniform for all students" (1972, p. 102). According to Guild, little has changed over the last 50 or so years. Regardless of the information we have about all the psychological processes that are involved in the brain's capacity to receive and interpret information, we continue to deliver a uniform program.

Students are subjected to the same books, the same formats, and the same pacing without any consideration of their backgrounds, basic knowledge, and developmental readiness for these materials. Compounding this strident uniformity, all students are tested at the same time with the same tests and compared, ignoring any differences inherent in the population. How can we ignore what we know about diversity in development, readiness, background, and cultures and continue along the same disastrous route?

Imperative to success for all is not only to examine the current structure expected for all students, but also to examine the disadvantages to those whose cultural beliefs and traditions do not easily digest the current norms emphasized in our classrooms. Finn and Freire criticize the differences in instruction according to class and socioeconomic strata. But have we gone too far in ignoring the cultural behaviors that have been taught in families and communities? Guild points out, "Students whose families value collaboration are told to be independent. Students whose cultures value spontaneity are told to exercise self-control. Students who are rewarded in their families for being social are told to work quietly and alone" (1998, p. 16).

The hypocrisy of what we know and what we practice has resulted in cultural conflicts that cause students to disconnect and withdraw from the current delivery of uniform instruction in school. Just as we know that individuals have different learning styles, must we acknowledge that cultural differences have a direct effect on assimilation of materials and a connection to education and learning? Teachers are aware that professional development programs come with prescribed strategies that are "proven" to be successful and are adopted by schools and districts for wide and uniform administration. These tools can be useful if they are allowed to be adapted to the diversity of other methods that best fit the student before them.

Thus, teachers should continue to gather strength in their areas of instruction. They need to examine the latest trends and research in methodology and delivery. But the most important area of study is the students themselves; their communities, families, beliefs, traditions, and individuality. The knowledge of how they learn and what is important to them will help them succeed academically and become part of a society where the good for the individual is the good for all. Yes, we can teach these children.

SUMMARY

The cultural differences that exist between the student, the community, and the teacher can have either an enlightening or calamitous effect, for student and teacher alike. The ability to enter the school community with an understanding of the cultural norms of that community will increase the chances of success for the student and the retention of the teacher. Expectations for behaviors that are culturally motivated and differ from expectations in classrooms can be a source of confusion for the student and consternation for the teacher. The sometimes different standards often cause conflict between what has been learned at home and what is expected in school.

Correction from school authorities causes a dissonance that might result in quiet submissiveness but internal resentment that would prevent the type of relationship that fosters mutual respect, learning for the student, and retention for the teacher.

In addition, the socioeconomic conditions that permeate the community and children's homes are crucial to understanding their developmental struggles in mandated programs and tests. Children who come from families that struggle daily to get food on the table and to pay the rent most likely have not had the stimulation that would ready them for formal instruction in the early grades. The lack of readiness, language acquisition, and familiarity with school-related materials in the early grades can compound problems and thwart cognitive processes throughout entire school careers. Developing programs and processes that allow students to achieve the required curriculum through individual needs assessment and support will increase the learning curve and help underprivileged students to reach their potential and mandated standards.

Teachers who are not attuned to the differences that affect learning can frustrate students and themselves in the educational settings in which they are placed. Teachers must learn about the community, know the circumstances of their students, and respect their traditions and cultures to succeed in the classroom. Retention and stability for schools, communities, and education in inner-city schools are determined by relationships based on mutual understanding and respect.

6

OVERCOMING STUDENT APATHY: ENGAGING STUDENTS IN HIGH-NEEDS SCHOOLS

Okonkwo had no more enthusiasm to plant his fields or gather his yams. He did only what it took to survive, to support his three wives and his children. He was no longer the great warrior that he had been in his old village. His spirit was broken; he had lost his drive and did not understand why his god had placed such a burden on him.

> His life had been ruled by great passion—to become one of the lords of the clan. That had been his life-spring. And he had all but achieved it. Then everything had been broken. He had been cast out of his clan like a fish onto a dry sandy beach, panting. Clearly his personal god or *chi* was not made for great things. A man could not rise beyond the destiny of his *chi*. The saying of the elders was not true—that if a man said yea his *chi* also affirmed. Here was a man whose *chi* said nay despite his own affirmation. (Achebe, 1994, p. 131)

Apathy is witnessed on all levels of society, albeit for different reasons. It has been described as either a submissiveness that encounters no motivation or direct rebellion against the prescribed standards of society. Americans have become more complacent and submissive, allowing those in power to dictate policy and social standards. Only in this last presidential election did we see some direction, enthusiasm, and determination. How long it will last, we will have to wait and see. The competitiveness that we once held as a society has diminished, and we are becoming the followers in the world of industry and technology. Thomas Friedman (2005) in *The World Is Flat* compares our ingenuity, drive, and competiveness with societies once considered our inferiors and puts us on notice to examine our industrial infrastructure as we continue to fall further behind in the global economy. His attention to the education of people in other countries and their accomplishments should provide impetus for improving our sense of urgency in all fields of endeavor.

Bob Compton (2007) examined the education systems in China, India, and the United States through a documentary, *Two Million Minutes*, comparing high schools in each of the countries searching for motivation, goals, and pathways of students getting ready to pursue their life's work. The lack of initiative and the laissez-faire attitudes of American youth are reported throughout the documentary, while the dedication and focus of the Indian and Chinese students to succeed are remarkable. Our educators are depicted as submitting to demands that are less rigorous and also submitting to pressures of standardized assessments that neither test knowledge nor challenge students to achieve higher levels of learning.

Standards of living in the three countries may hold one clue to the lack of urgency in the American student. Surrounded by the material necessities and in many cases luxuries that they have been accustomed to, they simply are not aware of how temporary those material comforts can be if we succumb to the notion that we are superior and always will be. In a discussion concerning student apathy, Yong G. Hwang (1995) wrote,

> Much of American society glamorizes easy success and the fast life. This cultural fashion has reached such a dangerous point that American children readily challenge authority and disdain intellectual development and achievement. . . . The effects of apathetic student attitudes on learning outcomes are profound. Foreign-born children of immigrants perform better than their US counterparts. Moreover, lax American student attitudes rub off on foreign-born students, as those who were born in America to immigrant parents do not perform as well (or study as hard) as students born in foreign lands. (p. 63)

Apathy is a noted presence in many schools across the country. Inner-city schools where students have struggled to succeed with prescribed programs and have experienced failure on mandated tests actively display a disconnection in the classroom. However, middle- and upper-income students who attend schools with more resources and qualified teachers have not escaped the apathy syndrome that is so prevalent in poor and minority-based neighborhoods. Although they pass the mandated tests and exams and even achieve scholarships and awards, they do not demonstrate the kind of competencies to compete globally.

When compared to other countries worldwide in science and math, the United States ranks 18th in the world, with an even more abysmal rank in literacy. Teachers in suburban schools with no poverty complain that parents refuse to accept responsibility if their child is not doing well and often blame the school or the teacher. The sense of accountability has been transferred to others with little thought to self. As one teacher explained, "My students express their apathy by simply telling me that they don't care." The behaviors in the classroom show the reaction to school and instruction; the problems are exacerbated with direct rebellion against the program and the teachers.

Kim and Eileen, math teachers in middle-school placements, state that their students are not at all shy at expressing their disdain for the subject or the tests that they are mandated to take. Eileen has students who have been placed in the low group and are especially difficult to motivate. As a matter of course, they are disruptive, uncooperative, and abusive to their classmates who choose to attend and participate. Kim complains that all attempts to make the material accessible to her students are met with questions like, "Why do I need to know this?"

Many students who are now in our middle and high schools have had years of failure in the school system. Haberman (1995) stated, "Most students in poverty become passive resisters after the primary grades and simply keep themselves from becoming fully involved in school" (p. 8). The question that needs to be examined is why they are apathetic and resistant and why they comply with the physical attendance policies but do not take advantage of the education they are confronted with. Students who attend many inner-city schools have environmental factors that affect the way they view the educational system. But apathy seems to be a general malaise in American schools, as evidenced by our standing when compared to schools around the globe, regardless of economic factors.

Too many of our students are satisfied with minimal accomplishments and do not see the advantages of hard work or effort within the school environment. The mentality of easy material prosperity and lack of understanding of the skills needed to obtain these goods has diluted the sense of the importance of learning. Teachers working in high-needs schools claim that students who live in poverty areas still have the latest sneakers, iPods, and cell phones. They see their students as competitive when it comes to possessions but not in achieving the best grade in school.

CASE STUDY: WHARTON AVENUE

Wharton Avenue High School is a citywide school with a population of approximately 2,400 students. The mission of the school is to prepare students for higher education, a two-year or four-year college, and for life in general. The school boasts a mission of "life-long learning and instilling the values of commitment, civility, hard work, honesty, and integrity. . . . An excellent education with unparalleled opportunity."

According to William, a teacher in the school, they strive to achieve academic success with understanding of the students' environments and to deal with each student in a compassionate and caring way. They encourage each student to give his or her own voice to the program and to become involved with choices for the program and future plans.

The school is comprised of seven houses or individual communities, which students choose when they enter the school in ninth grade. Each house has its own administration, counselors, and family coordinator. In addition, each house offers the major core courses and broad career choices. Personalized attention for each student is based upon need, from college preparation to assisting with abuse and homelessness. For students who have experienced trauma and exhibit extreme behaviors, social workers and other health officials are ready to intervene on the part of the student.

The extracurricular activities offer art, music, and sports programs to meet all interests in an attempt to involve students in one area or another. Teachers remain after school to tutor or give extra incentives in academic programs. The 21 percent of students who are classified as either learning disabled, emotionally handicapped, or in special programs are offered help outside of the school day.

Efforts by all who work at the school have had little effect on the success of the school and many of the students. The school earned an F in the 2006–2007 school year from the state of New York, and was ordered to reorganize and restructure for the next academic year. The population of the school comprises approximately 60 percent Hispanic and Latino, 30 percent black, 3 percent white, and 5 percent Asian or other. The low economic levels of the student are evidenced by the fact that 75 percent receive public assistance and 96 percent are eligible for free lunch. The average class size is 26 students, smallest being 11 and the largest 34. The attendance rate is 71 percent and the suspension rate is 16 percent. The graduation rate is approximately 50 percent, and in 2006, from that number, no student planned to go on to a four- or even two-year college.

In William's class of 29 students, he claims that only 15 come to school or attend consistently. The 50 percent attendance rate is an indication of the apathy that he sees among the student body. He reports that nearly 50 percent are so late for his first-period class that he finds it necessary to fail them. William's principal has expressed the necessity of passing students but he asks, "How can you pass students if they just don't try?"

The many partnerships put in place, the physical environment, the mission of caring along with the efforts at counseling, and the extracurricular opportunities have failed to motivate the students at Wharton High School. William reports an air of indifference among the majority of the population. The student population at the school has gained a reputation for being incompetent, lazy, and disrespectful.

The behaviors and attitudes of the student body have had a deleterious effect on the school as a whole. The teachers are becoming indifferent, many looking for positions in other schools. The students who have motivation are being affected by the majority and either follow the group mentality or drop out intellectually. The anti-intellectual attitudes and cultures of the school, the lack of discipline, and the displayed disrespect for the school and all that resides within are destroying the intent of learning and school. Hwang (1995) (citing Greenlee & Ogletree, 1993; Holfield & King, 1993) wrote, "Numerous studies indicate that, of a multitude of problems educators face, lack of discipline caused by anti-academic student attitude is the greatest factor which inhibits learning and school reform."

Student apathy is a condition that is prevalent in many schools and spans all populations and cultures in America. The interest in consumerism and entertainment permeates our society and is all encompassing. Students, once they have reached the secondary levels of education, are especially impressed with the attainment of goods. Consumerism, impressed upon society through the media, has become the most driving force with our students and our population as a whole. Solmitz (2000) proposed that "the consumerist inclination of our society is another factor that fosters apathy. We have become addicted to buy numerous products that we imagine make our lives easier and more appealing" (n.p.).

The availability of anything material and the desire or ability to purchase these items have been the motivators replacing intellectual pursuits or societal concerns. The short-sightedness of this consumerism is placing us in jeopardy of losing our influential position in the global economy. The effects of media, entertainment, consumerism, and material goals in particular are dominating students' attention and diminishing the need to learn and work.

CASE STUDY: BOBBIE

Bobbie has taught in two different settings in the inner city. She is currently a physical science teacher in Brooklyn and is discouraged by what she describes as students who are seemingly apathetic. Initially she attributed the apathy to the demographic composition of the students in her classes. She was aware of reported problems that seemed to pervade high-needs schools in the city. She thought perhaps they were not brought up to value education and its possibilities, or perhaps they did not have parents at home to encourage or help them with assignments.

Bobbie describes her students as uninvolved in each of her three science classes. Only a handful of students consistently turn in homework or pass class exams. Students' attitudes portray complete lack of motivation, failing even to turn in class work, have the necessary materials, or to take notes. Even when tests and exams are announced far in advance, students are still unprepared but outwardly undaunted when they receive failing grades.

Questioning her own techniques, Bobbie decided to make her lessons more student-centered, involving her students in some decision making in the format for the lessons. With new effort and research to make the lessons more applicable to their interests and levels, she saw little to no improvement. She states that despite her efforts to "cultivate better study habits and organizational skills and a sense of accountability in the class, students remained inattentive in class and test and quiz scores remained abysmal."

We contrast the apathy of those who have and those who have less in both experience and environment. According to Dewey (1995), "There are many meanings and many purposes in the situations we are confronted with. . . . Each offers its own challenge to thought and endeavor, and presents its own potential values" (p. 61). Those whose childhoods are long and difficult have more of a struggle to find the motivation necessary to see the possibilities in future endeavors.

If an internal oppression is felt by students who live in more impoverished environments and feelings of entitlement in students who live in more affluent environments, the results are the same. Students show a general sense of apathy in both circumstances but are more restrictive in the deprived environment.

But what are the circumstances that surround those who work in impoverished schools where excellence is demanded and achieved? What is the difference in these schools? How can we study their strategies and emulate their methods for other populations and other schools?

CASE STUDY: STEWART

Stewart works in a school in East New York. In 2006 the High School Official Review described the facility: the school is housed in an old building and its facilities are cramped and dated and unable to cope with the demands of the modern curriculum and instructional delivery. The facilities need upgrading and are not conducive to support effective teaching and learning for teachers and students alike.

Stewart's classroom is a good example of the condition of the building: "My classroom, room number 317, is the size of a large closet. It has two windows that take up the entire north wall; however, these windows do not allow sunlight to pass through and they open only halfway. The panes are not glass but fiberglass with no way to clean them. I teach three sections of English in this room and my average class size is 22. We have only four tables in the room and the students constantly complain of the size of the room and the smell. The language they use to describe the conditions is unprintable. One student even brought in a room freshener."

The majority of the 450 students who attend the school are not from the surrounding community but from boroughs all around the city. The demographics are half African American and half Hispanic/Latino. Most qualify for free lunch and the school has been designated as a Title I school.

What makes this poor facility a place for learning is the dedication of the young faculty. All have begun an effort to take each student to heart and establish relationships with them through extra "traditions" that show the students that they care about them as individuals and persons deserving respect.

Because of its small size and dedicated staff, they have been able to respond to some of the customs normally held by families in more stable environments. The teachers cook Thanksgiving dinner for all students, take them on field trips that they would not have the opportunity for otherwise, and stay after school until evening for homework help, special tutoring, and extracurricular activities. The teachers are not paid for this and thus show their care and concern for their students.

The staff began a community project that improved the school's appearance and appeal. They painted and cleaned the building, making it attractive and welcoming to all who enter. The results were that the school went from an F rating to a B in one year, with the goal being an A. The graduation rate has climbed from 1 student in 2000 to 90 students in 2008. The students' attendance rate has risen to over 90 percent and the curriculum is being aligned to meet the standards and the students' needs. What was once described as a facility that is not conducive to teaching and learning has become a place where students come to learn and strive.

SUMMARY

Apathy that is plaguing our educational system is at the root of our poor standing globally in academics and invention. We certainly cannot say that we are less intelligent or less able to achieve a competitive edge in all subject areas. We must act with urgency to begin a transformation from apathetic to motivated. Education is the priority for a rich and prosperous society. We can no longer ignore the poverty that plagues so many of our children, the poverty that ruins their health, their development, and their ability to learn. We must foster a sense of accountability from the family, the neighborhood, the community, and the nation.

It is important to build relationships and a sense of community that demand self-accountability from all constituents in the education system. The general public and the family are equal partners in the responsibility for education. Society as a whole needs to become intensely aware of the roots of apathy, take responsibility for that apathy, and develop attitudes of must do and can do without reserve and excuses that have plagued and undermined the purpose of education for all.

To begin our work toward positive attitudes and learning for our students, we need to look at those who have succeeded in the past and the present. What were their strategies? How did they overcome the difficulties in high-needs areas? How were the families of students engaged and partnered? We must overcome the problem lamented by Neikert (1991): "the disease in this country is the 'It's not me' attitude. It's never us, it's them, and that, them, is the nebulous array of unconsciously invented demons that prevent us from looking within, where the real fault lies" (p. 79).

The heroes of our education system, those who motivate and dispel attitudes of apathy, are the inward seekers who have the care and dedication to teach and learn. New teachers select education with great optimism, desiring to make a difference for children in society. The school can either stimulate and support this energy with vision and leadership or can quash the exuberance and destroy the future for these new teachers.

The apathy that new teachers meet in their classrooms and schools can be dispelled with support, caring, and courage, or they can become victims of the attitude, "It's not me, it's them."

7

MANAGING THE CLASSROOM: RELATING PUPIL BEHAVIOR TO ACADEMIC PERFORMANCE

New teachers have one challenge in common. They must all enter the classroom as newcomers, get to know their students, establish themselves as classroom managers and leaders, set the tone, fix the rules, and work out their complex relationships with their students—individually and in groups. Sound easy? It is one of the toughest things for a new teacher to do and accounts for why some teachers walk away, leave teaching, and find something else to do for a living. For as Lee and Choi (2008) stated, "good classroom management is believed to be 'an essential first step toward becoming a good teacher' (Ayers, 2001, p. 10)."

This chapter lays the groundwork for good classroom management (behavior, time use, proactive behavior), and shows, sadly, how weak teachers are sometimes unable to get control of things, find help from their supervisors and peers, and lose out. Simonsen, Fairbanks, Briesch, Myers, and Sugai (2008) put the case clearly: "Classroom management is an important element of pre-school teacher training and in-service teacher behavior, with three key parts: maximize allocation of time for instruction, arrangement of instructional activities to maximize academic engagement and achievement, and proactive behavior management practices" (see Sugai & Horner, 2002).

IN THE BEGINNING

Classroom management starts with the teacher's handling of the behavior of each student, and groups of students, but once established evolves into a whole set of behaviors and skills that define the very nature of teaching in the classroom. Ayers (2001) explained that handling kids is only the starting point, not the defining point, of good classroom management and teaching. As Lee and Choi (2008) wrote, "Ayers argues that this perspective about classroom management is one of the pervasive myths about teaching shared among professionals and the public and passed down for generations" (p. 495). Classroom management is more than handling kids; it focuses also on "the smooth flow of learning activities as well as daily routines" (Grant & Gillette, 2006, p. 99).

THE CASE OF WILL BRANT HIGH SCHOOL

This chapter, sadly, presents a case of a new teacher who was unable to get on top of the process and learn to manage the classroom and of course its students. The setting is one of the city's toughest high schools, William Brant, which is a particularly interesting place to look and to work. It is a beacon of hope to urban education—but a new teacher just did not make it through the first year successfully. While the goals of the high school are noble and high, Brant High School ranks among the worst in the city— among the "Dirty Dozen," although it shows some signs of rebounding. While on paper the school has improved, "in reality it has degraded student education and discipline to nothing more than a slip of paper," according to one teacher. Constant fighting, poor academics, and a constricting budget combine to make Brant High School an unhappy place to work.

Robin Baker (a fictitious name, real person), the first-year teacher described in this chapter, decided to try a first year at this school because her field advisor during teacher training had recommended it. Since her advisor, Mary Evans, was an incredible person and educator, Robin "quickly took up the teaching position there."

Brant High School has in its favor a good location—an urban middle-class neighborhood with fancy apartments and good shopping (although local families do not usually use the local public schools for their children); the building itself is clean and well maintained. The large high school only has one entrance, allowing the security guards to scan each student—a kind of "airport security," as the students call it. And the guards confiscate students' cell phones (Cooper, 2002) and other electronic devices.

Brant High School has 90 faculty, with a student-teacher ratio of 28 to 1, and an attendance office with about six staff. The school has separate cafeterias for teachers and students, and about half the students qualify for free and reduced-price lunch in the school. The building itself, it seems, was a former IBM factory, accounting for the good wiring, lighting, and Internet.

NEW TEACHER'S PERSPECTIVE

In a personal account, Robin Baker explains, "On a personal note, beginning from the beginning of school through to about October 30th, I have tried to meet with the principal every single day; I've had only one meeting with her. The teachers at Brant are a 'mixed bag'—some are hard-core, dedicated teachers, who really put in a lot of effort; and we have those who just take it as a job . . . and even have a few legally crazy teachers who by chance, cannot find another job anywhere."

Colleagues and the union in the school are not much help either. The teachers' union in the school is quite weak and gets little done, according to this new teacher. The principal is not forthcoming.

Robin is a change-of-career teacher who teaches math in the high school grades, with older students (ages 15 to 17) in 9th and 10th grades, and is in her second year.

Her first-period math class is a tracked lower-achieving group. She explains that her students rarely come to class on time; and when they do they are disruptive and noisy. She feels ready to leave the position because, in her words:

> I'm a bad teacher! I cannot control the behaviors of the students who are in my lower-track classes. They constantly disrupt my class; refuse to do their class work or their homework. And when I send these disruptive students from my class to the office, they are immediately sent back. I have tried to engage my students with fun, hands-on activities; but the students are unable to control themselves and participate.
>
> I've tried collaborative learning, modeling tasks for clarification, developing math vocabulary through games, and reciprocal teaching, to involve my students in the lessons. But they are unable to handle the activities, stay seated, and remain focused.

Robin, who has had some success with her other classes, finds this one unresponsive to anything she has tried thus far. Students come to class unprepared. They throw things at each other, jump over desks, and often quarrel and taunt each other. The few students that would like to learn have been completely overwhelmed and are beginning to copy the others' behaviors.

Robin believes that most of the students in this first-period class have indi-
vidualized education plans but she has not been privy to them, nor have they
been shared by any of the administration. She has tried to make sure that the
work that she gives them is more basic, trying to meet their needs. They get
upset at this work and will crumple or tear the papers. She has stated that all
she wants at this point is to get the year over with and survive this class.

POSITIVE FROM NEGATIVE

Polly is in her fourth year and her second placement. She is in Bushwick
and teaches ninth grade living environment. Her school, opened in 2003,
is the brainchild of two formerly disgruntled teachers who have formed a
collaborative atmosphere between administration and faculty. The school
has formed outside partnerships with the community and enjoys resources
and development from these partnerships.

The main thrust of instruction is reading and writing across the curriculum,
incorporation of social justice, and data-driven instruction. The demographics of the school are 70 percent Hispanic/Latino and 30 percent black; 86 percent of the students qualify for free lunch, making it a high-needs school.

In all three of her classes the students were uninvolved, rarely did their
homework, were never prepared for class, and were regularly failing their
tests and quizzes. They would become noisy and disrespectful, especially
on Fridays, quiz day. She at first began to make excuses for them—home
life, poverty, uninvolved parents, and lack of success in school. Now in her
fourth year of teaching and being much more familiar with the curriculum
and planning, she began a different tack for her students. She reflected on
her practice and found the following:

- She rarely returned corrected class work and homework.
- When students were absent she did not have a system where they
  could make up missing work.
- She had not developed a note-taking system for them to study from.
- They were not given organizational skills.
- She did not take into account that there was little support at home for
  them.

Her strategies were developed to include the following:

- She is always prepared and sets purposes for the lesson and the day.

- She developed a color-coded folder system for organization of student work.
- She disseminates a weekly assignment checklist, enumerating all assignments due at the end of a particular week.
- She uses daily note-taking templates to be used for assembly into the color-coded folders.
- She meets with students for extra help and tutoring.

What she has documented is an improved behavior and attention to class work. She has seen an increase in homework from 11 percent to 70 percent compliance, from 7 percent to 63 percent in class work, and test scores from 59 percent to 76 percent.

Polly continues to implement her strategies and sees better management for herself and her students.

CONCEPTS AND IMPROVEMENTS

These cases illustrate several of the key elements of good, positive classroom management and misconceptions that can lead to new teachers' frustration, failure, and withdrawal from teaching. While it is obvious in the case of Robin Baker that she should not have been given a tough, low-achieving class of poor children in the Bronx, at least not until she had matured as a professional, we see trends and axioms that might improve the practices of new teachers in working in their classrooms.

Reconceptualizing Classroom Management

The first step in understanding classroom management for new teachers is critical and should be clearly understood and used. First, classroom management is integral and connected to all teaching—as it goes on—and is not something a teacher does at the beginning of class ("sit down and keep quiet"). It is not about control but, as Lee Shulman (1992) so well explained, is "contextual, local and situated, requiring subtle judgments and agonizing decisions" (p. 28). Classroom management is really about being with students, getting them into the room, settled down, focused, and engaged.

At other times, teachers may confront what are called ill-structured situations and problems (Jonassen, 1997; Voss & Post, 1988), where good judgment, support, and experience come into play. Surviving the first year or two, as Robin and Polly found, is the key. Using their own opinions, new teachers need to work through the situation and pick up the techniques for speaking to and acting with their students. Sometimes called critical reflection, this may involve a number of steps that are important (see Slider, Noell, & Williams, 2006, pp. 218–219).

Building in Clear Classroom Instruction: Getting Children's Attention

The key part of classroom management is the instructional behaviors that begin with a focus, attention, and then requesting students to engage in learning. The teacher models the behavior, and is patient and gives the students time to respond. As Slider and colleagues (2006) explain, "Teacher states the child's name prior to issuing a request and/or child's face is oriented toward the teacher. Teacher then states on request and waits, without talking, helping the child, or threatening the child" (p. 218).

Modeling the Correct Response

Another step that principals might model to help new teachers improve their classroom management has been called case-based pedagogy and is useful and easy to carry out. As Lee and Choi (2008) explain,

> Unlike traditional in-service teacher training programs, *case discussions* encourage practitioners to change their views of authority from "formal, external sources to internal, collective sources" (Merseth, 1996, p. 733) where practicing teachers consider themselves "changer agents" and notice "wisdom in the group." (p. 502)

Thus, writing, discussing, and analyzing real cases of classroom behavior, management, and skills can really help new teachers to work on their techniques, thus developing repertoires of behavior and best practices using versions of reflective thinking.

Principals play a key role in making in-service and case-based learning opportunities available. How to organize these sessions and help teachers is the challenge for school leaders in working with the host of new and fast-track teachers in their first few years of practice.

Providing Guidance for the Child

Perhaps the most difficult but most critical step in becoming a new and quality classroom manager is the ability to relate to, communicate with, and help difficult students. With the extraordinary increase in the classification of children with special needs—reaching 16 percent nationally—and the tendency now to integrate these students into mainstream and regular classrooms, new teachers must be prepared to work in small groups and individually with these students as part of the teachers' management practices. Zuckerman breaks the steps in classroom management and discipline into three related stages or categories: (1) prevention, (2) managing common discipline problems, and (3) managing chronically disruptive children. The strategies for each of these—and they overlap and interact—are as follows (Zuckerman, 2007, p. 7):

- Prevention: Good lesson planning, preparation, and execution; clear classroom routines, rules, and norms; careful seating and rearranging of students for control.
- Managing common discipline problems: Being proactive by changing pace, nonpunitive time outs, interest boosting, redirecting off-task behavior, and giving cues to students before things get out of hand. More reactive interventions may involve nonverbal and verbal responses, and sequencing of the two.
- Managing chronically disruptive children: When being proactive, teachers should build relationships with students and work to break cycles of discouragement. Being reactive, when things break down, new teachers should learn to change students' seats, confer, and keep clear records.

The final and critical step is maintaining and improving the attention, behavior, and learning of children. Slider, Noell, and Williams (2006) have broken the management up into giving instructions by getting the students' attention, giving clear instructions, modeling a hint or prompt, and being patient (waiting 5–10 seconds after asking a question). Next the teacher gives guidance (even physically), and feedback with words or motions.

Praising the student is also important, contingent upon the child's behavior, specifically and sincerely, and with a variety of positive reinforcements. These classroom management skills are all important and should be explained, reinforced, and sustained by the school principal and other supervisors, if new teachers are to succeed. Principals play a key role as they support new teachers, and help and facilitate more experienced teachers in helping the newcomers.

Giving Clear Feedback

Finally, closing loops, giving good feedback, and recording results are all important and principals play a key role in seeing that information is collected, organized, and shared. As suggested, "Description of cases and situations can be collected for a case library posted on the individual school or school district website, making this library available to pre-service, novice, and experienced teachers so they can interact with and learn from each other's ideas, experiences, and perspective. In fact, the creation of the case library is key for good professional development" (Sullivan & Glanz, 2005, p. 14).

With the Internet, these situations can be made available, discussed, and used to help teachers and administrators to improve classroom management, instruction, and learning—and to help new teachers to survive and thrive. Teachers can demonstrate the best practices of organizing and working with students in the classroom, and other teachers can review and learn from these examples of best practices.

CONCLUSION

The future of education and the induction of talented new teachers who persist and grow in their jobs rest on researching and practicing the best methods for helping new teachers to manage their classrooms, for the benefit of both their students and their own professional and psychological well-being. These include: (1) "evaluating new classroom management strategies; (2) establishing both qualitative and quantitative standards for implementing classroom management standards by identifying the optimal ratio of positive to corrective consequences; and (3) specifying decision rules that guide the implementation of the continuum of consequences and instructional strategies—and when to move to more intrusive strategies" (Simonsen et al., 2008, p. 369).

We still have far to go in helping teachers to learn and perfect their classroom practices. We know that every little bit helps. Good teacher preparation, both fast and slow track; improved in-school, on-the-job orientation; and help from other teachers and administrators, who work closely with the teachers to help them. And teachers should never be afraid to talk one-on-one with disruptive students, for, as Zuckerman (2007) explains, "teachers should confer in private with their disruptive students to (a) pinpoint the specific problem behaviors, (b) identify appropriate behaviors, (c) check for the student's understanding, and (d) encourage a commitment for the student to improve" (p. 15). Remember, it is the behavior of the student that is bothering and disrupting the class and disturbing the new teachers—not the child (Ginott, 1972).

Lecturing new teachers on their practices, providing one or two workshops, and an occasional drop-in are not enough. New teachers, to grow and survive as professionals, need help and helpers, time to meet and share, opportunities to work with other teachers and the principal on becoming outstanding teachers—and surviving in the profession (Sugai & Horner, 2006).

It seems to us that with schools going high-tech and materials and recordings of teachers and students in their classrooms, that future training of teachers and ongoing staff development should go online with videotapes, modeling, didactic training, and other careful methods for helping new teachers (see O'Dell, Quinn, Alford, O'Briant, & Giebenhain, 1994; Sarokoff & Sturmey, 2004).

8

POOR RESOURCES
PLUS POOR EDUCATION
MEAN FEWER NEW TEACHERS

When taking a teaching job, particularly for the first time in a complex and changing profession, new teachers need resources to work on and work with. Starting a new job is like moving into a new home that is unfamiliar, poorly equipped, and unfurnished. All the classroom and school-site resources (e.g., equipment, handouts, books, computers, project materials, activity workbooks, and school building infrastructure—paint on the walls, lights in the ceiling) come together to create a classroom and school environments that have a profound effect on teachers, particularly nervous new ones. And new teachers may find poorly equipped, physically unattractive schools a real turn-off when trying to get started. As one teacher supervisor recently explained it, "Scarcity has been such a constant in education for so long that self-sufficient teachers routinely purchase classroom supplies at their own expense. Sometimes desperate measures are needed to obtain the most basic equipment" (Schmidt, 2005, p. 57).

Hence, resources matter, particularly for those in the classroom where teachers work and students learn. This chapter looks the physical world in the eye and makes concrete suggestions for driving more funds and resources to the teacher in the classroom.

The following are the words of a teaching fellow named Catherine, who had just finished the preparation program and arrived at her new post:

I was assigned as an NYC Teaching Fellow to PS 45 in Brooklyn. The conditions were deplorable. The building infrastructure was falling apart. There was pest infestation and there were barely any supplies. The library and the computer room were hard to book and there was no teacher support unless you were part of a network of teachers who had been there for over five years. I was given a class that was labeled "the lowest track" and spent most of my energies keeping my students under control. I had no support or avenues to supplies from those who were supposed to be the coaches in math, science, and literacy. My idea is that social studies can be the link to most subjects. We had no social studies material or curriculum that could be used as a guide. I left!

Maria teaches Spanish in Brooklyn. She states that her principal has spent money on professional development and has been annoyed with her because she has asked the presenter, "How can I implement your program when I do not have enough desks for my students? They have to sit on the windowsills, floor, or double up in chairs." Maria complains that in the winter they often have to wear mittens and hats because the heat is sporadic. She also has mouse infestation and cockroaches in her room. Materials are sparse and she spends her own money buying materials to make supplies for her classes. Maria is planning on moving to the suburbs.

RESOURCES MATTER

The problem of funding and resourcing schools, classrooms, and their teachers—old and new—has been around for decades, as educators and researchers were unable to determine how much of the funding in education actually reached the children (and their teachers) at the classroom level. We knew that education was growing, with more children attending schools for longer periods of time—and that the costs of education (and thus spending) were going up and up. But the finance models did not always exist for tracking dollars to kids, putting funds and resources in the classroom for direct instruction.

It was in the early 1990s that Cooper and Sarrel (1992) constructed and tested the finance analysis model (FAM), which functionalized the budget around actual uses and then decentralized the funds to school locations for children with different needs, such as special education and "regular" education. FAM looks like this, as a useful model for tracking dollars to kids for their direct education—and thus to the teachers, new and old.

In$ite—the Finance Analysis Model for Education—is software designed as an easy-to-understand information and finance reporting system for school district expenditures. For example, the state legislature in collaboration with the Rhode Island Department of Education has established a more detailed and informative system of reporting education expenditures for all school districts. This project was originally called Coopers and Lybrand or In$ite. (Fox River Learning, Inc., now owns the In$ite program.)

In$ite includes all sources of funding (federal and state grants, town or city general revenue funds, state aid, and other specialized funds that each district may receive) to analyze each district's expenditures.

With the millions of dollars being spent to educate our young people, it makes sense that decision-making data be available to district leaders, school leaders, and state leaders regarding where our resource dollars are being spent. In$ite is a system tool that helps greatly in this effort, as it provides consistent ways to review expenditures for every school district and in the near future for every school.

Every district's costs should not be the same—there are many policy and education program decisions for their particular student body that every district has the ability to make in the best interests of their students and with the resources available to them. In$ite provides a consistent method to look at the related financial information for each district.

How does the FAM group school district expenditures?

By Function

FAM categorizes funding into five functional areas, starting with direct instruction:

1. Instruction
2. Instructional support
3. Operations
4. Other commitments
5. Leadership

These functions provide a simple overview of how district funds are used to operate schools and to educate students. See below for details of each major function area. It is important that new teachers receive full funding at the beginning, so they can buy their materials and equip their classrooms. Instruction in the FAM model should be fully funded, and children in those classrooms who have special requirements should receive more funding.

Research on weighting the amounts based on the students might be useful here (see DeRoche, Cooper, Ouchi, & Brown, 2004): for example, if a new teacher has four classified special education children, five students whose first language is not English, and a few students from impoverished backgrounds, the schools should give greater fiscal weights to these special categories, which should translate into more resources (personnel and equipment) for these needy students. Money should follow the child, and benefit new teachers, for an investment in new teachers in the first few months can pay dividends for a lifetime, helping the new teachers to land on their feet.

By Educational Program

In$ite also assigns each expenditure to one of six broad program categories found in most school districts:

1. General education
2. Special education
3. Chapter I/Title I
4. Bilingual/ESL (English as second language)
5. Vocational education
6. Other programs

These programs provide a simple overview of the costs for each district's specific educational programs for their students.

By School Site and Grade Grouping Levels

FAM groups the same expenditure dollars described above (by function and by educational program) and also views them for each school location in a district. FAM combines dollars for individual schools into grade level totals for each district: elementary schools, middle schools, high schools, alternative schools, other schools.

What is included in each major function area? Each major function is divided into subfunctions and then into detailed functions. For example, the following list shows the divisions of instruction:

- Face-to-face teaching
- Instructional teachers
- Substitutes
- Classroom materials
- Pupil-use technology and software

- Instructional materials, trips, and supplies
- Instructional support

GETTING RESOURCES TO TEACHERS

The most difficult problem many new teachers thus face is getting started, getting set up, and making the arrangements they need to start their new profession. Here is a case of a school in a poor, ethnically diverse community in the Bronx that went out of its way to see that a new teacher, Christina, got off on the right foot.

Christina works as a technology coach in a grades 6–8 middle school in the South Bronx. Most of the students live in public housing and are mostly black and Latino/Hispanic. All teachers and students are grouped together in teams to form better relationships with the students. Technology is integrated into almost all aspects of the curriculum and instruction. Every classroom has a SMART Board with ongoing professional developmental support.

They have written and received a grant that gives a one to one ratio of laptops in the school. The teachers are using technology to improve reading instruction through differentiated texts, math instruction on the SMART Boards, and integrated instruction in all areas of the curriculum. Through hard work, ample supplies, and professional development, this school's staff have been invited to speak at nationwide conferences about their program. They are now in the process of trying to get the community online to improve communication and enhance their students' learning.

Here we see a case of strong social capital, as teachers were grouped and encouraged to work together, a particular benefit for a new teacher. Second, the school and classroom were high tech, which means SMART Boards and laptops for students and teachers alike. And third, the school and classroom were well funded, to the benefit of the new teachers. This level of site-based and classroom resourcing may require a better system of accounting and accountability. David (1994) in Kentucky found "that the biggest problem with the process of making allocations to school was the lack of appropriate accounting systems and technological support by school districts" (p. 711; see also King, Swanson, & Sweetland, 2003, pp. 445–448) to help schools and teachers to receive the funds they needed and to track the funding down to the classroom. For as King and colleagues (2003) explain:

> Tracing resource demands to the school and classroom level is essential for informed decision making in School Based Decision Making and Site Based Budgeting environments. It also has the potential, with appropriate analysis,

to enhance our understanding of how inputs affect education outcomes and equity in the allocation of resources. (p. 257)

Research and analysis thus indicate a number of models and perspectives for determining equity and availability of funds for teachers (Hyary, 1994). King et al. (2003) explain that specific school-level resources, the big step in getting more money to schools, and then to classrooms, included "average annual teacher salaries, percent of first-year teachers, percent of teachers teaching certification area, average number of students per class, number of microcomputers per 100 students, and number of library books per pupil" (p. 332). We would now include dollars reaching the classroom as a percentage of per-pupil spending by district or system and by each school; extra funding for special education, limited English proficiency, and other needs at the classroom level; and number of contact hours for students engaging in direct instruction and learning.

All of these measures are indicators of how well new teachers are being resourced and what materials and support they are getting in the classroom. Another newer indicator, too, is the recognition that children with different needs require different resources (often called weighted student formula or weighted student funding [WSF]). But again, we need some guarantee that teachers and their classrooms are getting a goodly proportion of these extra weighted funds—rather spending them all on outside resources, consultants, and hours of staff development. San Francisco Unified School District is using WSF, describing its advantages as follows.

One of the primary features of the WSF is that it allows school sites more flexibility than the previous system, called the staffing ratios model. Through staffing ratios, the central office basically directed school sites to spend the bulk of their resources in a particular way, through allocations of staff and a small supplies budget. This system gave schools little control over their financial resources. Under the WSF, each school site receives a budget denominated in dollars instead of positions and decides what staff and nonstaff items to purchase with those dollars. Under this approach, each school has more room to design and use innovative instructional programs that match the specific characteristics and needs of its students, parents, and community.

NEXT STEPS

From our analysis and case studies, we see six steps in resource allocation and use that can greatly increase the opportunity for new teachers to get what they need and to have control over materials, books, technology, and equipment in their classrooms.

Step 1: Explain budgeting and resourcing to new teachers. As we see it, new teachers (and many veteran teachers) may not understand how the money flows from the system to the classroom. With new technologies, new teachers can even look at the budget of their classroom, to determine what resources they are going to receive and might need.

Besides the usual new teacher orientation that is offered to staff, we also believe that budgeting and resources to the classroom should be reviewed every term, and teachers should be offered materials, books, software, and other resources whenever they indicate a need. This activity is a perfect opportunity to bring the superintendent, business management, tech support staff, and teacher mentors together around resources to reassure new teachers that they are getting what they need.

Step 2: Allocate adequate funding and materials to the school and classroom level to empower teachers in their work. Critical first steps in saving new teachers and helping them to survive are getting resources to them in their classrooms. Years ago, Berne and Steifel (1994) found that "an alarmingly low proportion of the general education budget for elementary and middle schools was reaching the schools" (King, Swanson, & Sweetland, 2003, p. 331). So reforms in resource allocation must start at the top with the system, the budgeting, and the accounting systems that inform school leaders and teachers about what resources they receive, and then move downward to the department, grade level, and teachers and their classrooms.

Step 3: Use site-based budgeting in all schools, to empower the teachers and administrators to meet the needs of all students. Brimley and Garfield (2008) make it clear that for the improvement of quality of schools and the support of their teachers, new and senior, funding and budgeting should be school based. As they explain,

Site-based budgeting (SBB) is a concept of developing a district budget through the involvement of teachers [yes, importantly, new teachers], community, and administrators at the school level. The process provides an opportunity for the school staff to assist in building a budget that will have an impact on the final decisions made by the board of education. It is a decentralized system of providing revenues for instructional supplies, materials, equipment, texts, library books, and in some districts, is extended to salaries for teachers, aides, custodians. (p. 313)

The benefits that Brimley and Garfield (2008, p. 314) present for site-based, and now classroom-based, decision making can be summarized as follows: (1) influencing school policies; (2) improving morale and teacher motivation; (3) strengthening school-site planning and resources; (4) fostering effective schools; and (5) ultimately, improving student achievement (see Malen, Ogawa, & Kranz, 1990, p. 32).

Step 4: Give principals more control and encourage them to fund new teachers more generously and appropriately. Every new teacher should receive a grant from the district to buy materials and get set up. Principals are the key players who should work closely with the new teachers to introduce the concepts of site-based decision making and classroom-level budgeting.

As one new teacher explained:

> I am now in a school that embraces social studies and uses it as a link to teaching and learning literacy. At Public School 43, we study Central Park in the spring and birds in the fall. We live the study. We have materials to read about the connections, and we build our own park model out of recycled materials and write our own guidebooks and maps. We have ample materials and produce an end product that is used as an assessment for literacy and social studies.

Step 5: Keep new teachers in close touch with more senior teachers, who can be encouraged to share their resources and skills. It seems clear, too, that mentor teachers can loan and give new teachers more resources and equipment to get them started. Sharing is part of being a good colleague, and sharing resources can make a big difference to a new teacher who talks into a dark, empty classroom and needs everything to get started. While team teaching is almost gone, teamwork is not.

Lausberg (1990) saw the need almost two decades ago for site-based funding and control when he explained that the "purpose of site-based management is to give the principal and instructional staff [and new teachers too] more control over budget, personnel and organization at the school level. The concept's objectives are: greater involvement in decision making, less imposition of state or district level rules which restrict creativity or school-level choices, and the development of innovative instructional methods which will ultimately improve education results and the adjustment and longevity of new teachers in their school settings" (p. 11).

In all, good information, greater autonomy, and more useful resources together will help new teachers to adjust to their jobs. And the future lies in technology: computers and software to help teachers teach and students learn. We have only seen the beginning of the ed-tech world, and students are learning to text message and communicate with each other. These resources may help teachers to work together, sharing ideas and methods, and help them teach better. Herein lies the future.

Step 6: Meet and interact with new teachers regularly, to ensure that they are settling in and have the help and resources that they need. It seems clear from this research, and others, that being there, being involved, being alert, and making resources available through the first few years are all essential to saving new teachers and helping them to grow and improve.

Schmidt (2005) put it nicely when he wrote: "Finally, remember that you have the power to create an atmosphere of appreciation and *abundance* for teachers in a famine culture. By honing a repertoire of skills to recognize, reward and motivate your staff [and new teachers], you will reap a rich harvest of [new] and renewed professional enthusiasm" (p. 15).

Teachers having resources is always about the school's leadership garnering and managing finances well. The FAM shows us how to bring the money down to the school and classroom, making transparent the funding of the school and teachers. Once the funds are in the school, and then allocated to the classroom, new teachers need to see their own ability to get and use money (and materials) to their benefit.

While resources alone will not and cannot ensure a happy, productive first years as a teacher, one can bet that having a rundown school, with shabby classroom desks, tables, and equipment, and limited materials (and now classroom technology), will make that first year into a hell.

9

LESSONS LEARNED: INITIATING AND SUPPORTING QUALITY TEACHERS AND SCHOOLS

Schooling is the very foundation of our democracy and worldwide bid for leadership. In a world where we currently hold the bottom quartile of educational excellence, if we are to believe the reports, it is time to look at what education is and whom it affects. The relationship of schools to society and different socioeconomic status of people is paramount to our success as a society that promotes itself as one based on fairness and social justice. Just as we began to complete this book, the financial standing of the United States crumbled. Millions of people have lost their jobs, many financial institutions have fallen, corruption has been revealed, and life as we knew it has changed, perhaps forever.

Politics is once again playing its power game at the expense of education; but on the brighter side, education is one of two professions that are still in need of staff. Even while the power play between the two major parties has cut the education budget by $16 billion dedicated for repairing the infrastructure of deteriorating school buildings, we have the opportunity to recruit from a larger and larger constituency of possible new candidates for our classrooms.

Perhaps, as Thomas Friedman (2005) suggests, the hierarchies of power jobs are being leveled and the attraction to the teaching profession will increase and become understood as the basis of our very sustenance and freedom. Friedman writes about the collaboration and cooperation of high-tech companies and industries around the world sharing knowledge to advance quality and excellence in communications and connective ideas. He credits their success with the erasure of the strict lines of hierarchy and bureaucracy, allowing all to communicate and connect.

RECRUITING AND SUSTAINING NEW TEACHERS

Is this, then, our opportunity to recruit and retain highly qualified people to the schools with the most need? Can we blur the lines of bureaucracy to allow creative ideas to flow and become less constrained by unwarranted mandates? Using the platform of the flat world, can we become more collaborative and connected globally to improve our instructional delivery, using the best from all?

The experience that we have learned from personal case studies and histories of teachers within a system can and should be used to help us understand the complexities of working in our diverse schools. Colleges and universities are instrumental in implementing and maintaining current knowledge of successful methodologies but must include pluralistic values and understanding of the cultures and diverse needs in schools. Social policy and theory must include the rights and expectations that the cultural groups we teach will have differences from our own customs and traditions. It is imperative that we respect the idea that even while maintaining their cultural differences they are part of one society and share the opportunity for both political and economic stability and power. Beck (2005) confronts pluralism as an "outlook linked to the belief . . . that there is no ultimate foundation to life, that knowledge . . . including moral knowledge . . . is conditioned by changing human interests and traditions. Different communities and interest groups construct values to suit their particular needs and customs" (p. 199).

UNDERSTANDING CULTURAL DIFFERENCES

Prospective teachers must examine their own biases in teaching and learning and become familiar with the communities they are about to enter. Most new teachers in fast-track programs are white and have themselves been educated in upper- or middle-class white majority schools, where collaboration and exploration through constructivist methods were employed. Others from Asian and African backgrounds were educated in a strict and rigid environment where competition and respect for authority were part of the expectations. It is, in fact, not what they learned but how they learned that they bring with them into their classrooms.

Behaviors that have been instilled in us from early in our development must be brought to consciousness in order to examine stereotypical responses to the other. At the same time, teachers need to recognize that those same behaviors that impressed us as children are also influencing the behaviors of the students in classrooms. Jean Moule (2009) sums it up: "Examining and revealing our own levels of conscious intent is imperative to actually understanding our biased behavior . . . to become less focused on feeling very tolerant and good about themselves and more focused on examining their own biases" (n.p.).

Colleges and universities should also include courses of study that address the needs and beliefs of diverse communities. Mastery of the curriculum, while important, is by no means the most important when teaching students with backgrounds different from the teachers'. The manner in which most of our new teachers learned can be quite different from the customs of family and community of imparting and receiving information.

Most new teachers who come to teach in the inner city come with an objective of helping or giving back. Some come through fast-track programs to get their degrees and quickly leave, but most do not. It is up to them to navigate communities that are unfamiliar to them, develop relationships with the leaders of those communities, learn the customs and traditions, and respect the diversity that exists within their schools.

LEADERSHIP

Leadership in the schools can make or break the retention of the new teacher. Supporting new teachers by giving them the materials and mentorship they need helps establish comfort in a new and unfamiliar environment. Establishing trust is vital for the administrator in order to ensure success in the classroom, school, and school community. The integrity of the administration is displayed through continued support in difficult situations and unwavering honesty in dealing with all staff in the building. When faculty and staff distrust the principals in a school, a chaotic climate can be discerned, a lack of cohesiveness, and an enervated feeling by staff and students alike. Likening the role of the administrator to feelings we can all relate to, Bennis (1989) asserts:

> Imagine how our national cynicism about politics would change if we found our elected officials to be honest, fair and competent, not to mention forward

looking. For "honest" we may read consistent. Consistency is the likelihood of trust. People who do what they say they say they will do—meet their commitments, keep their promises—are trustworthy; those who don't aren't. Most of us prefer to be led by someone we can count on, even when we disagree with him. (p. 21)

Disillusionment with the system can be a direct result of experience with an ineffective and unauthentic principal. He or she is the primary person who establishes either a can-do or can't-do attitude in a school. In today's schools where mandated tests and reporting are a fact of life, principals can increase or decrease the natural tensions that are inherent in this mandated system. Using the results of standardized tests as the form for teacher evaluation is not only unfair but ignores all the variables that influence test results on a given day.

Enthusiasm for a school, its students, and the community is a direct result of the principal who understands her community and assists her new teachers to do the same. She is informative, supportive, and communicative, and provides feedback both positive and negative to assist in the growth of the new teacher. Even without adequate supplies or extra monies, realistic motivation can be infectious and result in teachers remaining to do the work they first dedicated themselves to.

Rewarding teachers' efforts even while they are struggling through their first years establishes a positive and accepting attitude. Corrections and suggestions for improvement are more easily accepted when they are nonthreatening and directly focused on progress. Providing staff development directly related to the classroom is an enhancement that helps new and inexperienced teachers to establish program and routine in their classroom. The process of responding to teachers' needs and assisting them in renewing both their knowledge base and commitment to teaching will result in a more rewarding experience and retention in the profession and the school.

Principals and other administrative leaders should examine their process for academic achievement and social interaction in the school community. If the goal of the school is to promote success and meet the rigid standards set by a bureaucratic system, inclusion of staff is the only opportunity for realization. Through planning and decision making that is inclusive, validation of staff is achieved, ideas are shared, common ground is established, and support becomes visible and conclusive. Teachers invited to be part of the decision-making process become physically, intellectually, and emotionally connected to the school and are more likely to remain.

PEER COLLEGIALITY

Schools are social institutions where collaboration and problem solving are the means to success. Burnout is a common term used to signify a teacher's inability to either cope or remain actively engaged in the teaching and learning process. What are some of the causes of burnout? Classroom teachers work alone in their rooms, isolated from other peers in the building for periods of time. They are, for the most part, responsible for handling all the circumstances that occur within the classroom environment. This can be daunting, lonely, and doubtful.

New teachers are especially prone to feel the effects of physical, emotional, and psychological drain from the day-to-day confrontation of pressures and problems. They have been exposed to theory, course work, and supervised student teaching; or, for fast-track teachers, only four weeks in a summer school program before they enter the realities of the classroom. They are often not prepared to meet the demands of the program, the mandated assessment expectations, or the physical strains of classroom life.

Large schools with populations that range from 800 to 2,500 students do not give principals and other administrators the time to mentor and support their new staff. And due to the culture of isolation pervasive in the structure of schools, Harris (1995) asserts that "schools present few opportunities for teachers to engage in sustained professional dialogue about their learning and their teaching" (p. 54). The feeling of being completely overwhelmed and unsuccessful in their quest to teach results in many new teachers leaving the profession after one year or after their obligation is completed. Principals need to see that each new teacher has a mentor and confidant to share their frustrations and to use as guides through the first critical days and year of teaching.

Levin and Ammon (1992) suggest "that the process of becoming a teacher does not cease at the end of formal training but continues into the induction year and beyond." The ability to collaborate and problem solve through a mentor or the team approach relieves much of the anxiety and provides the daily support needed in the first years of teaching. As documented through the case studies, teachers who were able to join a collaborative effort and become peers had more of a tendency to feel part of the school and are planning to remain in their placements no matter the population of students they are teaching. With access to forums that facilitate professional and problem-solving strategies, Babinski and Rogers (1998) found "that the new teachers' emphasis on 'self as teacher' was evident throughout the year and that the consultant groups provided the teachers with a forum for engaging in meaningful professional dialogue with colleagues" (p. 285).

OVERCOMING APATHY

The assessment reports that are published every year show some students excelling in our schools, but for the most part we are looking at average to mediocre scores on tests from 4th grade through 12th grade. Just getting by seems to be the standard that is set by the student and accepted by schools as long as they are not labeled as failing.

Have we blurred the line between what education is and what feels good for society? Have we lost our enthusiasm to be competitive in the world; are we content to just be?

Student apathy can be attributed to many markers in society and must be recognized as a national instead of just a local problem. We know that crumbling schools with mice and roach infestation, peeling paint, and general disrepair are not the environments that promote the importance of learning. We know, too, that poor leadership and revolving doors for teachers and administrators do not show students the dedication to education so often preached. And we know that a home where the importance of learning is not stressed is a negative influence on learning. Thus physical conditions, the lack of stability in school staff, and lack of encouragement from home are all contributing factors to apathy.

According to Yong G. Hwang (1995), American schools are experiencing student apathy across the socioeconomic spectrum. Hwang attributes the increasing apathy and lack of learning zeal to a society that "glamorizes easy success and the fast life . . . governed by the anti-achievement dogma which glorifies defiance and ridicules academic interest" (p. 2). This would seem to be documented in the comparison of global achievement where we are, at best, in the lower 25 percent in literacy, math, and science.

The documentation and criticisms of our schools has been an ongoing debate since the publication of *A Nation at Risk* in 1983. The government has attempted to improve student outcomes through a variety of movements and legislative programs. The result has been disappointing, with student achievement continuing its mediocre to poor showing nationally. Remedies that have been attempted include merit pay for success, prescribed programs and curriculum design, bonuses to families to get their kids to school, No Child Left Behind laws designed to increase scores through yearly testing, and summer institutes for remedial work.

We certainly have the intellectual capabilities at the least to be competitive and at the best to meet the world with the strengths of scholarly leadership. Pockets of success in inner-city and suburban schools need to be studied for their visions and implementation of policy and program. Why do students in these schools succeed and continue their pursuit of higher education and learning? Is there a secret to motivating even previously apathetic students toward motivation and excitement in the teaching and learning process?

Ted Sizer and Nancy Sizer (1999) wrote a book, *The Students Are Watching*, that emphasizes the influence of adults in the lives of children from a young age up through high school and provides the perfect segue into a case study that is current and powerful.

CASE STUDY: MATT

Matt works in an inner-city school in New York City. The school is relatively new and has had the opportunity to develop a program for students in grades 9–12. The school houses a population that is minority based; black, Hispanic/Latino, and Asian. Students are not selected but come from neighboring communities. The poverty level is high, as indicated by the more than 85 percent free lunch recipients. The principal is a transformational leader. Her curriculum is designed with input from all staff members and any parents who would like to participate; most have not to date.

A dean who is visible and consistent monitors discipline in the school. Most serious infractions are handled with a remand for community service. Students who are disruptive are removed from the classroom, allowing the teachers to attend to their main objective, teaching. There are mentors for new teachers and a principal who both supports and shows value for her staff. Meetings are held to look at programs and issues regarding student achievement. Teachers are encouraged to engage in research and innovation, while remaining constant to the standards and state mandates.

Matt is a second-year fast-track teacher who believes that his students, while in the average class, can achieve at the honors level. He has begun a project to assess current levels of proficiency and has begun a program that is building from the students' current levels to the honors expectations. The students are excited and eager to prove their worth and to follow the lead of their teacher. Support from his colleagues and principal and eagerness for the outcome have proven exciting for all. The students are seeing and mirroring the excitement of the adults and to this point are meeting the expectations for success at the honors level.

Apathy may be created for a variety of reasons but the power of the school can be the instrument that turns the apathetic child into one who is motivated and hopeful. As Marion Wright Edelman (2008) professes,

> Teaching has to be more than a job; it has to be a calling . . . you can have the best equipped school, smallest class size, and a great curriculum, but if teachers and principals do not love children, children will know it and be hurt. . . . Teachers must be committed to finding and nourishing the gifts in each child and to building the child's sense of confidence and competence. . . . Children must achieve and those entrusted with educating must perform. (pp. 21–22)

CLASSROOM MANAGEMENT

We see from Chapter 7 that classroom management is an initial hurdle for new teachers: how to relate to students, build trust, encourage cooperation and participation, and avoid seeing management as strictly control and punishment. Alfie Kohn (1996) reacted to a suggestion made by a teacher that a program called assertive discipline was a substitute for good classroom atmosphere and management. Kohn wrote, "my stomach reacted the same way hers [the teacher's] did to the sight of marbles in a jar, or a hierarchical list of punishments on a classroom wall" (p. 11). He saw this kind of program, assertive discipline, as "a collection of bribes and threats whose purpose is to enforce rules that the teacher alone devises and imposes"— getting the "train to run on time in the classroom, never mind whom they run over," to use Kohn's words (p. 11).

In summary, Kohn wrote: "To help students become ethical people, as opposed to people who do merely what they are told, we cannot merely tell them what to do. We have to *help* them figure out—for themselves and with each other—how one ought to act" (1996, p. 15). And teachers, new ones in particular, are no different. They need to learn more than rules and regulations for their classrooms. They need help from colleagues and supervisors in establishing activities (engaging ones) in their classes, getting students working together and learning together. New teachers cannot easily survive alone. They need colleagues who care, and places to talk and visit, and observe—to learn the tricks of the trade and to get help when they need it. Building a classroom that is organized, productive, and well managed is the main first step in getting started as a new teacher.

RESOURCES

Helping new teachers to grow in their jobs requires resources: equipment, books, computers, materials, and time from other professionals (commonly called staff development and improvement). We know that many school systems lack the budgeting technology and models to make spending transparent and to drive more resources down to classrooms and teachers. While site-based management, budgeting, and decision making have been around for at least 20 years, we are still not sure that new teachers are given the funds and resources they need, when they need them.

It is the main responsibility of the principal to see that new teachers have what they need, in a timely fashion. Odden (1992) put the package together when he argued for school-based funding, coupled with school-based management. As he explained, "The school would be the primary recipient of local, state, and federal revenues. The school then would budget the funds, determining the mix of professionals—teachers, administrators, adjunct [and new] teachers—at the school site, and to hire, supervise, promote, and fire them. . . . In short, the proposed structure would have real site-based management and real site-based budgeting" (p. 333; see also Clune & White, 1988). This empowering of the school and its principal and staff would at least give new teachers access to resources that they need, rather than having to apply to a district system with a principal's help.

Thus, once the school and its leadership have control over resources, it increases the chances that funds and materials will be made available to new teachers, who will have money to buy equipment, new computers (one for each child, one can hope), books, and other materials, to help set up shop and make the classroom work.

MAKING THE MODEL WORK

Ultimately, the skills and resources, human and otherwise, should be brought to bear to the advantage of new teachers, to help them survive, grow, and stay in their schools. Fast-track programs, like Teacher for America and the NYC Teaching Fellows Program, are critical examples of programs to help urban districts replace aging teachers. While this process will likely slow in this economic environment, since teachers may not be able to retire or leave urban schools since jobs are getting tougher to find, we still will see turnover and the need for new teachers of quality for many years to come.

As shown in figure 9.1, this process again requires the Six Rs of good leadership at the school level. The purpose is clear: to recruit quality new teachers, and to retain them, by responding to their needs as learning professionals; rewarding them when they make progress, requiring close collaboration and supportive supervision. And reviewing their work on an ongoing basis, while helping them in renewing their courage and determination to survive and to grow as new professionals. The dynamics of the Six Rs are critical if new teachers are to make it.

THE FUTURE

What does the future hold? As thousands of teachers consider whether to retire or stay, the recruitment and retention of new teachers will continue to be a concern in education. This book has looked at cases and examples of ways to help new teachers and offers strong suggestions for making schools a better place for orienting, supporting, and mentoring of these new teachers.

Other concerns are on the horizon. For example, how can schools orient and support whole groups of teacher replacements and new teachers within the traditional school? Second, the demography is changing, as more older, second-career staff are hired, creating two cohorts of the typical newer, younger teachers, alongside a host of more mature newcomers, perhaps more rigid teachers who bring with them their values, practices, and beliefs based on years of work outside the education field. How will schools and universities handle cohorts of new teachers with ranges in age, backgrounds, and experience? Surely the traditional student teaching and new-school orientations may not work for everyone. Education leaders

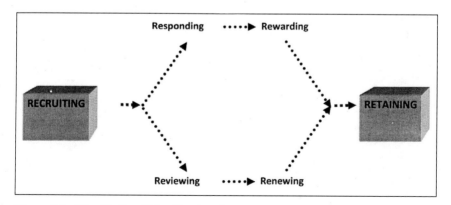

Figure 9.1. The Six Rs of New Teacher Retention

need to explore various support and orientation programs, specific to the age group and the requirements of a range of new teachers.

Third, we suggest a longitudinal study of new teachers, tracking their progress over three to five years, to see how well they progress, for those who stay more than a year or two. How well do new teachers—older and younger—adjust to the culture of the school, and the diversity of the students, their families, and the broader community? For example, if former investment bankers, with master's degrees in business from quality universities, decide to become teachers, how might the school and students benefit from their experiences and abilities? And how might those experiences translate into quality teaching, the ability (or not) to relate to students of color, students from poor families, and immigrant children?

Thus, younger new teachers, while they lack the experience, may be more flexible and may relate better to younger students; but on the other hand, a group of more mature new teachers may be better role models for their students, who may lack accessible middle-class, middle-age role models and supports in their community.

Thus, education is being reborn, as a new generation of teachers comes into our schools. These new resources are critical to the future; but they also present a challenge to teacher-training institutions and to schools where these neophytes first go to work. The time is right for new methods, new ideas, and new approaches. For example, Schumaker and Sommers (2001) explain that change may work, or not, as "trailblazers make a small group of teachers or administrators who will try almost anything. They are the ones who go off to a conference, or workshop, and return ready to totally change their program or the whole school at a moment's notice, as long as it sounds like an improvement" (p. 81). Saboteurs may be teachers who resist change, and according to Schumaker and Sommers (2001) may inhibit change "when they are confronted with a different way of doing something" (p. 81).

Taking a more collaborative approach, a school leader working with new teachers should create peer support and collegiality through, for example, study groups that examine best practices. This process will offer new teachers support on an ongoing basis during those critical years. Thus, creating an open, two-way communication system—between new and experienced teachers and between teachers and administrators—should help new teachers to adjust and survive, and go on to become outstanding educators.

Furthermore, we need to pay closer attention to the preservice training of new educators, to meet the needs of new teachers in preparation for helping more diverse students. "Educators at all levels today must be prepared to meet the needs of increasingly diverse student populations, with varying learning styles, family situations and beliefs about what schools mean for them. . . . Four or five years of undergraduate preparation, regardless of the quality, will never be sufficient to prepare educators for careers in a field as dynamic as education" (Guskey, 2000, p. 275). In particular, Guskey wrote: "The changes we seek can be accomplished only through continuous, on-going, job-embedded, high-quality professional development. And clearly, the best way to ensure this quality is through continuous, on-going, high-quality evaluation of programs" (p. 275).

Thus, the lessons learned in helping new teachers to adjust can also be adopted for helping experienced teachers to improve and renew themselves. Good environments, strong leadership, and creative approaches have the potential for helping everyone in the school—and the new teachers will benefit and perhaps survive to teach another day. As George Bernard Shaw explained, "The reasonable person adapts himself to the world; the unreasonable one persists in trying to adapt the world to himself. Therefore, all progress depends on the unreasonable man." Thus, nurturing new teachers, as difficult as it is, may be a stimulus for improving the environment, culture, activities, and all professionals in our schools, becoming a motivator for change, rather than a burden. Let us hope so.

REFERENCES

Achebe, C. (1994). *Things fall apart*. New York: Anchor Books.

AERA Autumn Division A, Leithwood, K., & Riehl, C. (2003). *What we know about successful school leadership*. Chicago: AERA.

American Youth Policy Forum. (2002–2003). *Annual report: Every nine seconds in America a student becomes a dropout*. Washington, DC: Author.

Atkinson, J. (2007). Teaching Fido how to whistle. Summer Leadership Conference, Asheville, NC.

Ayers, W. (2001). *To teacher: The journal of a teacher* (2nd ed.). New York: Teachers College Press.

Babinski, L. M., & Rogers, D. L. (1998). Supporting new teachers through consultee-centered group consultation. *Journal of Educational and Psychological Consultation, 9*(4), 285–308.

Beck, J. (2005). *Cognitive therapy for challenging problems: What to do when the basics don't work*. New York: Guilford.

Bennis, W. (1989). *Why leaders can't lead: The unconscious conspiracy continues*. San Francisco: Jossey-Bass.

Berne, R., & Stiefel, L. (1994). Measuring equity at the school level: The finance perspective. *Educational Evaluation and Policy Analysis, 16*(4), 405–421.

Brimley, V., Jr., & Garfield, R. R. (2008). *Financing education in a climate of change* (10th ed.). Boston: Allyn and Bacon.

Cantor, N. (1972). *Dynamics of learning* (2nd ed.). New York: Agathon Press.

Clune, W. H., & White, P. A. (1988). *School based management: Institutional variation, implementation, and issues for further research*. Rep. No. RR-008. New Brunswick, NJ: Rutgers University, Consortium for Policy Research in Education.

Compton, B. (2007). *Two million minutes: A documentary on global education.* A Broken Pencil Production.

Conger, J. (1996). *The human side of school change* (R. Evans, Ed.). San Francisco: Jossey-Bass.

Cooper, B. S., & Lee, J. W. (2006, July 15). Cellphones in schools? *Education Week, 25*(42), 44.

Cooper, B. S., & Sarrel, R. (1992). Managing for school efficiency and effectiveness. *National Forum of Educational Administration and Supervision Journal, 8,* 3–38.

Counts, G. (1995). Dare the schools build a new social order. In W. Kohli (Ed.), *Critical conversations in philosophy of education.* New York: Routledge. (Original work published 1932.)

David, J. L. (1994). School-based decision-making: Kentucky's test of decentralization. *Phi Delta Kappan, 75*(9), 706–712.

DeRoche, T., Cooper, B. S., Ouchi, W. G., & Brown, C. (2004). From courtroom to classroom: Operationalizating adequacy in the funding of teaching and learning. *Educational Considerations, 32*(1), 19–32.

Dewey, J. (1995). Pragmatism: The aims of education and the meaning of life. In W. Kohli (Ed.), *Critical conversations in philosophy of education* (pp. 42–55). New York: Routledge. (Original work published 1950.)

Dewey, J. (2004). *Democracy and education.* New York: Kessinger. (Original work published 1916.)

Dillon, S. (2009, April 7). Report envisions shortage of teachers as retirements escalate. *New York Times,* p. 54.

Du Bois, W. E. B. (2006). *Cultural deficit theory.* Westport, CT: Greenwood.

Edelman, M. W. (2008). *The sea is so wide and my boat is so small: Charting a course for the next generation.* New York: Hyperion.

Erikson, F. (1987). Transformation and school success: The politics and culture of educational achievement. *Anthropology and Education Quarterly, 18*(4), 335–356.

Evans, R. (1996). *The human side of school change: Reform resistance, and the real-life problems of innovation.* San Francisco: Jossey-Bass.

Finn, P. (1999). *Literacy with an attitude.* Albany, NY: SUNY Press.

Ford, D. Y., & Whiting, G. W. (2008). Cultural competence: Preparing gifted students for a diverse society. *Roeper Review, 30*(2), 104–110.

Freire, P. (1970). *Pedagogy of the oppressed.* New York: Continuum.

Friedman, T. (2005). *The world is flat.* New York: Picador/Farrar, Strauss and Giroux.

Fullan, M. (1991). *The new meaning of educational change.* New York: Teachers College Press.

Ginott, H. (1972). *Between teacher and child.* New York: Peter H. Wyden.

Glassman, N. S., & Glassman, L. D. (2007). *The expert school leader: Accelerating accountability.* Lanham, MD: Rowman & Littlefield Education.

Glickman, C. D., Gordon, S. P., & Ross-Gordon, J. M. (2007). *Supervision and instructional leadership: A developmental approach* (7th ed.). Boston: Allyn & Bacon.

Goodlad, J. (1976). *Facing the future: Issues in education and schooling* (J. S. Golub, Ed.). New York: McGraw-Hill.

Goodlad, J. I. (1984). *A place called school.* New York: McGraw-Hill.

Goodlad, J. (1987). *Ecology of school renewal.* Chicago: University of Chicago Press.

Grant, C., & Gillette, M. (2006). *Learning to teach everyone's children: Equity empowerment, and education that is multicultural.* Belmont, CA: Thomson Wadworth.

Greenlee, A. R., & Ogletree, E. J. (1993). *Student apathy, lack of self-responsibility and false self-esteem.* Chicago: Chicago Board of Education.

Guild, P. (1994). The culture/learning style connection. *Educational Leadership, 51*(8), 16–21.

Guild, P. B., & Garger, S. (1998). *Marching to different drummers* (2nd ed.). Alexandria, VA: Association for Supervision and Curriculum Development. Available from http://www.ascd.org/publications/books/.

Guskey, T. R. (2000). *Evaluating professional development.* Thousand Oaks, CA: Corwin.

Haberman, M. (1995). *Star teachers of children in poverty.* West Lafayette, IN: Kappa Delta Pi.

Harris, A. (2005). *Improving schools through teacher leadership.* New York: McGraw Hill.

Hess, R., & Shipman, V. C. (1965). Early experience and the socialization of cognitive modes in children. *Child Development, 36*(4), 869–886.

Holfield, M., & King, D. L. (1993). Meeting the needs of beginning school administrators: Report of a professional induction project. *Journal of School Leadership, 3*(3), 321–328.

Hoy, A. W., & Hoy, W. K. (2006). *Instructional leadership: A research-based guide to learning in schools* (2nd ed.). Boston: Allyn and Bacon.

Hwang, Y. G. (1995). Student apathy, lack of self-responsibility and false self-esteem are failing American schools. *Education, 115.* Available from http://www.questia.com/googleScholar.qst?docId=5000341123.

Hyary, A. (1994). Intra-district distribution of education resources in New York State elementary schools. Paper delivered at the American Education Finance Association meeting, Nashville, TN.

Isenberg, J. (1994). *Going by the book: The role of popular chronicles in the professional development of teachers.* London: Bergin & Garvey.

Johnson, S. M. (2001). Can professional certification for teachers reshape teaching as a career. *Phi Delta Kappan, 82*(5).

Johnson, S. M., & Kardos, S. M. (2002). Keeping new teachers. *Educational Leadership, 59*(6), 13–16.

Jonassen, D. H. (1997). Instructional design models for well-structured and ill-structured problem solving learning outcomes. *ETR&D, 45*(1), 65–94.

Kennedy, M. (1998, April). The relevance of content in in-service teacher education. Paper presented to the American Education Research Association, San Diego, CA.

King, R. A., Swanson, A. D., & Sweetland, S. R. (2003). *School finance: Achieving high standards with equity and efficiency* (3rd ed.). Boston: Allyn & Bacon, Pearson Education.

Kohn, A. (1996). *Beyond discipline*. New York: Prentice Hall.

Kouzes, J. M., & Posner, B. Z. (1987). *The leadership challenge: How to keep getting extra-ordinary things done in organizations*. San Francisco: Jossey-Bass.

Kozol, J. (2005). *The shame of a nation: The restoration of apartheid schooling in America*. New York: Three Rivers Press.

Ladson-Billings, G. (2001). *Crossing over to Canaan: The journey of new teachers in diverse classrooms*. San Francisco: Jossey-Bass.

Lausberg, C. H. (1990). Site-based management: Crisis or opportunity? *School Business Affairs, 56*(4), 10–14.

Lee, K., & Choi, I. (2008). Learning classroom management through web-based case instruction: Implications for early childhood teacher education. *Early Childhood Education Journal, 35*(6), 495–503.

Levin, B. B., & Ammon, P. (1992). The development of beginning teachers' pedagogical thinking: A longitudinal analysis of four cases. *Teacher Education Quarterly, 19*(4), 19–37.

Lortie, D. (1975). *Schoolteacher: A sociological study*. Chicago: University of Chicago Press.

Malen, B., Ogawa, R. T., & Kranz, J. (1990). Unfulfilled promises: Evidence says site-based management hindered by many factors. *School Administrator, 47*(2), 30–59.

Marzano, R. J., & McNulty, B. (2003). *Balanced leadership: What 30 years of research tells us about the effect of leadership on student achievement*. Aurora, CO: Mid-Continent Research for Education and Learning.

Merseth, K. K. (1996). Cases and case methods in teacher education. In J. Sikula, T. J. Buttery, & E. Guyton (Eds.), *Handbook of research on teachers education* (2nd ed., pp. 722–743). New York: Simon & Schuster Macmillan.

Moule, J. (2009). Understanding unconscious bias and unintentional racism. *Phi Delta Kappan, 90*(5), 44–48. Retrieved from http://www.pdkintl.org/kappan/k_v90/k0901mou.htm.

Munby, R., Martin, H., Russell, T., & Martin, A. K. (2001). Teachers' knowledge and how it develops. In V. Richardson (Ed.), *Handbook on research on teaching* (4th ed., pp. 877–904). Washington, DC: American Educational Research Association.

National Commission for Teaching and America's Future. (1996). *What matters most: Teaching for America's future*. New York: Author.

Neikert, W. (1991, June 23). America is the land where everything is somebody else's fault. *The Buffalo News*, p. H8.

New York State Teacher Certification Examinations Web page. (2008). http://www.nystce.nesinc.com.

Odden, A. R. (1992). Toward the twenty-first century: A school-based finance. In R. Odden (Ed.), *Rethinking school finance: An agenda for the 1990s*. San Francisco: Jossey-Bass.

O'Dell, S. L., Quinn, J., Alford, B. A., O'Briant, A. L., & Giebenhain, J. E. (1982). Predicting the acquisition of parents' skills via four training methods. *Behavioral Therapy, 13*, 194–208.

Patri, A. (1997). From *A schoolmaster of the great city*. In R. M. Cohen & S. Scheer (Eds.), *The work of teachers in America: A social history through stories*. Mahwah, NJ: Lawrence Erlbaum. (Patri's original work published 1917.)

Ravitch, D. (2003). A brief history of teacher professionalism. *White House Conference on Preparing Tomorrow's Teachers*. Retrieved from http://www.ed.gov/print/admins/tchrqual/learn/preparingteachersconference/ravitch.

Ravitch, D., & Viteretti, R. (2000). *Left back: A century of failed school reforms*. New York: Simon and Schuster.

Quirk, K. (2008). Dr. Martin Haberman: Haberman's career dedicated to quality public education. *The Haberman Educational Foundation*. Retrieved from http://www.altcert.org/DrMartinHaberman.aspx?sm=a2.

Sarokoff, R. A., & Sturmey, P. (2004). The effects of behavioral skills training on staff implementation of discrete-trial teaching. *Journal of Applied Behavior Analysis, 37*(4), 535–538.

Satow, J. (2005, June 20). *New York Sun*, p. 1.

Sawchuck, S. (2009). Stimulus bills spurs focus on teachers. *Education Week, 28*(24), 1, 18.

Sayas, A. (1996). To grow a teacher. *Basic Education*, 40.

Schmidt, L. (2005). Chalk is cheap: Nurturing teachers in a famine culture. *Principal, 84*(3), 57–59.

Schumaker, D. R., & Sommers, W. A. (2001). *Being a successful principal: Riding the wave of change without drowning*. Thousand Oaks, CA: Corwin.

Shulman, L. S. (1986). Those who understand: Knowledge growth in teaching. *Educational Researchers, 15*(2), 4–14.

Shulman, L. S. (1992). Toward a pedagogy of cases. In J. H. Shulman (Ed.), *Case methods in teacher education* (pp. 1–29). New York: Teachers College Press.

Simonsen, B., Fairbanks, S., Briesch, A., Myers, D., & Sugai, G. (2008). Evidence-based practices in classroom management: Considerations for research to practice. *Education and Treatment of Children, 31*(3), 351–380.

Sizer, T., & Sizer, N. (1999). *The students are watching: Schools and the moral contract*. Boston: Beacon Press.

Slider, N. J., Noell, G. H., & Williams, K. L. (2006). Providing practicing teachers classroom management professional development in a brief self-study format. *Journal of Behavior in Education, 15*(4), 215–228.

Solmitz, D. (2000, November 4). The roots of apathy and how schools can reduce apathy. *Local Voices Online.* Available from http://www.rem1.org/local_voices/summer2000/education/apathy.htm.

Sugai, G., & Horner, R. H. (2002). The evolution of discipline practices: School-wide positive behavior supports. *Child and Family Behavior Therapy, 24*(1–2), 23–50.

Sugai, G., & Horner, R. H. (2006). A promising approach for expanding and sustaining school-wide positive behavior support. *School Psychology Review, 35*(2), 245–259.

Sullivan, S., & Glanz, J. (2005). *Supervision that improves teaching.* Thousand Oaks, CA: Corwin Press.

Tozer, S. E., Violas, P. C., & Senese, G. (2002). *School and society: Historical and contemporary perspectives.* New York: McGraw-Hill.

Vogel, R. K. (Ed.). (1997). *Handbook of research on urban politics.* Westport, CT: Greenwood Press.

Voss, J. F., & Post, T. A. (1988). On the solving of ill-structured problems. In M. T. H. Chi, R. Glaser, & M. J. Farr (Eds.), *The nature of expertise* (pp. 261–285). Hillsdale, NJ: Lawrence Erlbaum.

Zuckerman, J. T. (2007). Classroom management in secondary schools: A study of student teachers' successful strategies. *American Secondary Education, 35*(2), 4–16.

INDEX

ABOUT THE AUTHORS

Janet D. Mulvey is assistant professor at Pace University School of Education in New York City, and has formerly served as a school principal for 13 years and teacher for over 7 years. Her interests include the study of politics and policy in education and school improvement in urban settings.

Bruce S. Cooper is professor of educational leadership at Fordham University and former president of the Politics of Education Association. His interests include labor relations, school finance, and school policies.